C000091141

www.iconfilms.co.uk

OUTDOOR LIVES SERIES

Beautifully Grotesque Fish *of* *the* American West

Mark Spitzer

UNIVERSITY OF NEBRASKA PRESS
Lincoln and London

Chapter 1 was originally published in serial installments
as "The American Eel: An Aquatic Phantom in
Arkansas," in *Sporting Life Arkansas* in 2014. The
website *Only in Arkansas* republished this version in
2014 (onlyinark.com/sports/American-eel-arkansas-
aquatic-phantom). Chapter 2 was originally published as
"Making Environmental Lemonade with the Creature
that Put the 'Ish' in 'Fish,'" in *Saltfront*, no. 1 (Summer
2014), and as "Burbot Bash: Chasing the Creature
that Put the 'Ish' in 'Fish,'" in *Frontiers* (Spring 2014).
An abbreviated version of chapter 7 was broadcast
on NPR's *Tales from the South* in September 2014.

Publication of this volume was assisted by a grant from
the Friends of the University of Nebraska Press.

Library of Congress Cataloging-in-Publication Data
Names: Spitzer, Mark, 1965–, author.
Title: Beautifully grotesque fish of the
American West / Mark Spitzer.
Description: Lincoln: University of Nebraska
Press, 2017. | Series: Outdoor lives series |
Includes bibliographical references.
Identifiers: LCCN 2016024935 (print)
LCCN 2016048655 (ebook)
ISBN 9780803265233 (cloth: alk. paper)
ISBN 9781496200044 (epub)
ISBN 9781496200051 (mobi)
ISBN 9781496200068 (pdf)
Subjects: LCSH: Fishes—West (U.S.)
Classification: LCC QL628.W39 S65 2017 (print) |
LCC QL628.W39 (ebook) | DDC 333.95/60978—dc23
LC record available at https://lccn.loc.gov/2016024935

Set in Janson by John Klopping.

Contents

Illustrations

BEAUTIFULLY GROTESQUE FISH

OF THE AMERICAN WEST

Introduction

In Wildness Is the Preservation of
the Grotesque and Vice Versa

If I didn't write this book, I'd have two questions about the title. First, what's the definition of "Beautifully Grotesque"? And second, where exactly is the American West? But since I did write this book, and since others may have the same questions, that's where I'll begin, starting with the geographical question.

The Mississippi River, of course, runs right down the middle of the country and, for centuries, has been historically regarded as the eastern border of the West. Even before the pioneers, this metaphorical dividing line between what used to be seen as *the known* and *the unknown* has essentially served as a symbolic gateway to "the Frontier." And since the fish I know best are to the west of this river, and since this river's role as the edge of the West is a firmly established theme in American literature (as in Huck Finn lighting out "for the Territory"), I chose this boundary, like many others have in the past, to define the western states.

The idea, however, that the West represents vast expanses of wilderness that are rich in possibility is a bit antiquated now that the teeming cities and industry of the East have migrated west, homogenizing the entire country. Thus it may be too simple to continue to think of the East and West as representing *the old* and *the new*—or, as Henry David Thoreau once pictured this contrast, as *civilization* vs. *the Wild*. These extremes are considered in his essay "Walking," in which he writes, "We go eastward to realize history and study the works of art and literature, retracing the steps of the race; we go westward as into the future, with a spirit of enterprise and adventure." Thoreau also writes, "The West of which I speak is but another name for the Wild . . . in Wildness is the preservation of the world"—with which I agree in principle. But as just noted, I'm not convinced that our romantic ideas about the West are as definitive as they used to be.

I've been using these Thoreau quotes for the last fourteen years in the environmental courses I regularly teach, and they work well for introducing college students to the question of America's western identity. I follow the Thoreau discussion by asking students to brainstorm what represents the West for them, and I write their answers on the board: mountains, cacti, cowboys, Indians, wagon trains, prairie dogs, the Grand Canyon, Wall Drug, the Gold Rush, oil wells, mind-numbing drives across Nevada, etc. These are some of the typical responses, but there's still a defining characteristic that's part of the modern discussion but usually escapes being mentioned. So I give them a hint: that it's more of a lack of something than a presence—and somebody usually gets it.

Water is a natural resource that everybody everywhere needs to survive. As I point out in my eco-classes, we couldn't have established this country from coast to coast if we hadn't found ways to harness this resource and exploit it for our national expansion. I bring this up in order to move on to the *Cadillac Desert* documentaries that examine how we founded major cities in hostile environments, created water wars between competing states, constructed a highly complex system of levees and dams and channels for irrigation, and commenced a history of both sanctioned approaches and guerilla tactics to preserve our natural heritage.

But in that classroom moment focused on defining the West, and especially in Missouri, where I began teaching this perspective, the eyes would start to roll. Basically, the students were skeptical of water being so important. That is, until I'd ask them to name one natural lake in the state. I'd receive a bunch of responses, but then I'd explain that natural lakes are formed by glaciations, which lakes in Missouri never had. "Sure," I'd go on, "there are oxbows and sinkhole ponds." But according to the Missouri Department of Conservation, those don't count as natural lakes. As for the rest of the lakes in Missouri, those are all reservoirs. Because these days, part of what defines the American West is our consciousness of water, which is something we take for granted, as if it's always been here and will always be here. As if all we have to do to get some is turn on the faucet. Then I'd drop the bombshell by telling them that because of our water use, Missouri is the American West.

The students would look around at one another, clearly out of their comfort zone. Seeing themselves as lifelong midwesterners, they were always reluctant to accept this hypothesis just because some professor had a crackpot theory. And when I moved to Arkansas and gave college students a similar spiel, the reaction was the same. Having identified themselves as southerners all their lives, it didn't compute for some northern professor to tell them they were westerners.

But the thing is, under this definition of the American West, we're all becoming westerners. Water is scarcer, toxic spills are on the rise, the aquifers are compromised, and there are water shortages right now in states like Wisconsin, where rivers and lakes abound and there's even a Great Lake.

My point being this: freshwater fish live in fresh water, and the freshwater fish of the American West, which have been dealing with water issues since the 1800s, are now dealing with accelerating problems. And just as we are all becoming westerners in terms of our relationship with water, so are our fish. And by "our fish," I don't just mean American fish. I'm talking about all our fish, from the Mississippi to the Mekong. Because the fish of the American West (our paddlefish and sturgeon, for example) are metonymic for other fish that will soon be facing what our western fish are currently facing, if they aren't dealing with those issues already (like overfishing, acidification, habitat loss, invasive species, petro-chemical contamination, synthetic hormones affecting gender, etc.).

The environmental aspect of this book, however, is only part of the equation. On one hand, my intention is to suggest solutions, but on the other, I made it my mission to have a blast catching at least one of each species profiled in this book, no matter the size. And I'm glad to say I accomplished that goal—even if I did fudge a bit in catching a burbot by dumpster-diving in Utah.

Although this book was written for a general audience, and for a specialized readership of biologists, educators, fishery managers, and other conservationists, it was envisioned primarily for people like me, who love to fish, and think about fish, and who ultimately tend to end up stuck in the mud waiting for a tow truck because of fish. Because fish provide adventures for us. Because fish aren't just barometers of what is and isn't in the water; they also measure our quality of life.

But to get back to the question of what "Beautifully Grotesque" means—well, the answer is that I've long been attracted to the monsters and mutants in our waters. Give me your wretched, your maligned, your demonized—this has always been my motto. Ever since I saw my first alligator gar in a fish book at the age of six, I've been fascinated by the weirdest creatures in our midst, the ones we often label grotesque.

Catching a beat-up bowfin as a kid or a bulging one-eyed carp always gave me an adrenaline rush, one that surpassed the awe of landing a crappie or bass. I grew up netting inner-city bottom feeders in the creek across the street, drawing aliens with barbels and fins, and storing moments in my head, like when Huck and Jim landed a possible world record river cat but had to forgo bragging rights because they were on the lam.

Then when I got to college I immersed myself in a more formal study of the grotesque, the subject being the Medieval and Renaissance wild man, a half-human character running shaggy through the woods, swinging a club and fighting knights. As a research assistant for an actual Dr. Savage, whose scholarship focused on these mythical creatures, I scanned more than a million images in the Marburger Index (a microfiche archive of art throughout Germany) looking for wild men and wild women in illuminated manuscripts, on church pews, on tombstones—you name it. The result was a four-hundred-page senior thesis on the significance of wild people in art history and literature, for which I received a grant to travel through Europe with a photographer to find and document more images of this particular pagan grotesque.

But my heart, really, was with the fish. I kept after them, and the uglier and more disgusting they were, the better. I pursued them to the point that in graduate school, my master's thesis became a novel about a misunderstood, man-eating catfish. That thesis, later published as the novel *Bottom Feeder*, was highly influenced by the monkeywrenching philosophies of Edward Abbey, and it concerned a cast of whacky characters fighting to preserve a fictionally extinct grotesque.

Since then I've researched and published two books on the loathed and reviled gator-headed gar—a fish that is frequently considered a grotesque, like the gargoyle. But I've also written other novels full of grotesques (like apocalyptic hybrid freaks and crazy Alaskan leviathans) as well as collections of investigative verse that examine legendary grotesques in Arkansas, not to mention the bizarre and grotesque hellbender salamander.

But to label my interest in the grotesque a fetish would be misleading. I'm not interested in what our imaginations picture as gross or scary because I get off on celebrating a childlike wonder for the fantastic. I'm interested in fish with faces that only a mother could love for the same reason I chose to research the most obscure texts I could find by the French authors Jean Genet, Arthur Rimbaud, Louis-Ferdinand Céline, Georges Bataille, and Blaise Cendrars (who, incidentally, were all obsessed by the grotesque). Basically I went looking for their most unsung and dismissed works, because I saw opportunities in translating texts with a bastard status (e.g., fragments of verse, lost letters, ignored plays, and other works not usually considered "legitimate"). My objective wasn't just to beat somebody else to publishing those books, but to take those works out of the shadows and cast them in another light, so that they could be appreciated for their unique and overlooked literary value.

Hence this book, in which I combine science, folklore, history, ecology, and imagery, then stitch those aspects together with first-hand experiences that come from pursuing underwater underdogs. And luckily for me, the action is set in the American West, a place I've known and loved all my life—from traveling cross-country as a kid, going to grad school in the Rockies, and living in a van and camping my way through the deserts and plains, researching translations in special collections up and down the West Coast, bonding with the waterways of Louisiana, Minnesota, and every western state where I fished and worked and visited family and friends, and cutting through Omaha and Kansas City and Denver and Reno and Salt Lake City to continue my lifelong study of the grotesque in Arkansas.

That's where I began this book by proposing to editor Matthew Bokovoy that his interest in noodling (or hand-fishing) and my passion for investigating fish commonly considered "ugly" could result in an action-packed portrait of eleven remarkable species. Matt had faith in this vision before I even knew the specifics, and he went out of his way to shepherd the project to completion. I'd like to thank him for that, as well as editor Heather Stauffer, the manuscript readers, the Board of Directors, and all the other staff members at the University of Nebraska Press involved in the production of this book. You did an amazing job!

I'd also like to thank Casey Cox of the U.S. Fish & Wildlife Service for taking me electrofishing and sharing his research, as well as my trusty sidekick Scotty Lewis, who helped me catch Malvern the American eel. My acknowledgments as well to Wyoming Game and Fish Fisheries Supervisor Robert E. Keith for responding to questions on burbot, and Brian Raymond of the Chamber of Commerce in Manila, Utah, for connecting me with local experts and providing information on the 2014 Burbot Bash in Flaming Gorge Reservoir. Bartek Prusiewicz was an excellent and amusing guide, and I thank him and Lars Larsen for taking me sturgeoning in Oregon. Eric Tumminia, aka Hippy, and Steve Kahrs of L'Osage Caviar, aided in my examination of paddlefish and provided some key perspectives. In Kansas, Jessica Howell, Jessica Edmunds, and Chris Steffan of the Kansas Department of Wildlife, Parks and Tourism were generous enough to take me cruising on the Kaw for erupting silver carp, and I'm deeply appreciative. Thanks also to Daryl Bauer of the Nebraska Game and Parks Commission for giving me last-minute directions to his office in Lincoln and staying late for the arrival of the state record yellow bullhead. Also, thanks to Dr. Randy Jackson at Cornell University for clarifying the approximate age of the bowfin family and to professional photographer Rob Butler for braving vipers and impaling limbs when we took part in the Okie Noodling Tournament.

Regarding photographs: It turned out that I had way too many to incorporate into this book. For those who would like an extra fix of the grotesques, I plan to publish additional photos in my series *Where in the West Is Mark Spitzer* on the University of Nebraska Press blog. One can therefore go to the UNP blog to view full-color pictures that illustrate other parts of the overall story of what went into this project.

I'm grateful to have received support from the Estate of Ernest and Emma Spitzer, which made it possible to finance the brunt of research in this book during the worst semester of my life. It was a time when I absolutely had to get out of town, so I was fortunate also to receive a sabbatical from the University of Central Arkansas for fish research, which allowed me to rediscover my connections with the American West. UCA contributed travel research funds for northern pikeminnow and oversized sturgeon in the form of a summer stipend, which was imperative support for this book.

Thanks go to my Fishing Support Group: Rob "Turkey Buzzard" Mauldin, Ben "Minnow Bucket" Damgaard, and the aforementioned Scotty "Goggle Eye" Lewis, who saved the day in chapter 7. Still, Turkey Buzzard deserves the most credit, for continuously letting us make fun of him.

A number of professional fishing guides lent their expertise, including Dawson Heffner of Texas Megafish Adventures; Kevan Paul in Clear Lake, Iowa; Gabe Schubert in Stillwater, Minnesota; Josh Stevenson of Mighty Musky Fishing Guide Service in Oakdale, Minnesota; Mark Christianson and Jeff Woodruff up on Leech Lake in Minnesota; Skipper, JoAnn, and Christian Bivins of Big Fish Adventures, LLC, out of Temple, Oklahoma; Steve Brown of Catfish Safari in Warsaw, Missouri; James Nichols on Lake Norfolk, Arkansas; and Jason Schultz from Hell's Canyon Sport Fishing in Idaho.

Paul Marsh, Brian Kesner, and Jamie Wissenal from Marsh's Native Fish Lab in Arizona contributed greatly to this book. Ben Head at Ana-Lab Corporation in Kilgore, Texas, and chemist Jacob White in Ohio were also important to its evolution, and so was author Scott Foster, who took me out for northern pikeminnow on the Columbia River. Eric Winther and Scott Mengis from the Washington Department of Fish and Wildlife were key in getting a handle on this fish. Dr. Solomon David at the Shedd Aquarium in Chicago helped out whenever I had a question involving primitive fish. Dr. Leigh Graham (also known as the poet Lea Graham), proved the most important player in this odyssey for me, and I thank her for the optimism she inspired in this project and beyond.

Then there are the journal editors who published versions of various chapters in *Frontiers Magazine*, *Saltfront*, *Arkansas Sporting Life*, and *Only in Arkansas*. A version of the noodling chapter was broadcast as well on NPR's *Tales from the South*; thanks to Paula Martin Morell and her team for that, and to my colleagues in Creative Writing at UCA for recommending me to represent our faculty, since this platform allowed me to articulate publicly a controversial yet necessary observation on destructive fishing practices for genetically jumbo flathead cats.

I dedicate this book to fishing support groups and *pescadoras* everywhere, as well as to the spirit of Wildness that has always defined the American West. This fierce and resilient quality is still embodied in our most beautifully grotesque fish—which persevere in our nightmares and dreams, despite our constant abuse.

Mark Spitzer, Arkansas, 2016

I

Nature of the American Eel

An Aquatic Phantom in Our Own Back Yard

When I showed up in the parking lot, Casey Cox was out by the dumpsters, looking a lot less gnomelike than when we sampled alligator gar a year earlier. I'd seen this transition to the clean-cut look before with a few of our biology grad students at the University of Central Arkansas, especially when they're looking for jobs, like the internship Casey had recently scored. It was the perfect position for him, since he was studying American eels, and the local U.S. Fish & Wildlife Service (USFWS) office was responding to a push to list this creature as an endangered species.

A blond, good-natured navy vet in his late twenties, Casey was catching eels all over the state. He was collecting data for his thesis and working on an "eel ladder"—which is what these serpentine squigglers need to get beyond the dams that have been blocking migrations throughout their range.

American eels are usually associated with the Atlantic Coast and the river systems that enter the continent east of the Mississippi; their distribution extends from the coastal streams of Greenland to the northern shores of South America. But they also occur in the West. Swimming in through the Gulf of Mexico, they're in every state along the Mississippi River, plus Texas and South Dakota. They used to exist in New Mexico, they've been recorded in Arizona, they were introduced in Utah and

California, and they escaped from a facility in Colorado. They're also in Nebraska, due to a railroad bridge collapsing in 1873, spilling a load of eels into the Elkhorn River.

Sometimes traveling up to ten thousand miles, they have the greatest known range of any fish in North America (and yep, they're actual fish, with tiny slimy scales). They're born in the Sargasso Sea somewhere between the Bahamas and Bermuda, and being "catadromous," they eventually head into fresh water, where they live for three to as many as forty years until they're sexually mature. That's when they head en masse back to their unknown spawning grounds to get it on and die.

"Howdy," I greeted Casey.

We shook hands, and he showed me a tub filled with nine American eels between eight and twelve inches long. Right above the water line there was a six-foot tube of PVC pipe set at a forty-five-degree angle, heading up to a fifty-five-gallon barrel. Casey was pumping water up to it, the water was flowing down, and there was a length of "substrate" going through the tube consisting of wire mesh and nylon netting material. Basically, this was an eel ladder.

An eel came up to the surface with its elongated spade-shaped head. It peeked into the opening, squirmed a few inches in, then backed out.

"They're thinking about it," Casey said, "but there's probably too much light right now."

It was an early afternoon in May, and being nocturnal, eels are used to hunkering down during the day, hiding under rocks and logs. They do this throughout a third of the country, and hardly anyone ever encounters one—which is something I find staggering. Like millions, I've spent most of my life amidst these fish but have never caught one, or glimpsed one, or even heard of anyone catching one. It's as though they're figments of our imagination—or aquatic phantoms appearing whenever they please.

But that's the main thing about eels: they've been mystifying humans for centuries, thanks, in part to philosophers like Aristotle positing a bunch of bunk. He claimed they arose from the "entrails of the sea." Then came Pliny, who wrote that they rubbed against rocks and the goo that came off turned into juveniles. Eventually a medical student named Sigmund Freud took a more scientific look. He spent weeks dissecting the American eel's European cousin in hopes of writing the seminal study on their testicles. Unable to find these, he moved on to psychology. Go figure.

Another eel came undulating up, and I commented that it must be a she to be so far upstream, since the males stay closer to salt and brackish water. Casey agreed and mentioned that sexual differentiation occurs at between thirty and forty centimeters. Before that, they're all "intersexual," meaning they can go either way. According to a USFWS report from 2007, gender is most likely "influenced by environmental factors, including eel densities." When densities increase, so do males. When densities decline, so do females. The more lakes there are in an area, the more females there are as well, which tend to grow larger than the males—sometimes up to four feet long. Ultimately the genders join up when they're ready to breed, and the whole eely exodus heads out to sea.

An eel entered the tube and we cheered as it wiggled up, but then it stopped halfway. Another one entered. Then another. Something was driving them to follow the flow. Or maybe they just wanted to get out of the light. Whatever the case, they remained in there and refused to venture all the way up.

Casey said I could take one, and not too long after that I went home with a bucket. Digging through my mind for the most ludicrous, non-eely name I could think of, I decided on "Fire Hydrant." I dropped my new pet into an aquarium set up in my office. The observations had begun.

After being eggs and larvae, eels go through four more life cycle stages. Fire Hydrant was a "yellow eel," and she definitely had a champagne sheen. Mostly, though, she was olivine-gray with a bright white belly.

The juveniles are referred to as "glass eels," because they're transparent. They enter this stage when about six centimeters long, and then they metamorphose into "elvers." This stage lasts three to twelve months, during which they try to evade catfish and bass. Ultimately the survivors become "silver eels" and assume a much more muddy color. Their wrap-around fin becomes even larger, and if you catch one big enough to eat, all you have to do is fillet it like a catfish. A commercial fisherman once gave me one, and it wasn't fishy tasting at all. I grilled it with some olive oil and paprika, and the meat was white and sweet.

Fire Hydrant, however, had disappeared the morning after I brought her home, getting away through a gap the size of three dimes stacked on top of each other. When I pulled back the desk, I could see water splattered against the wall, and then her tail beside the baseboard. I grabbed her and she was still alive, so I put her back into the aquarium, figuring eels must have lunglike organs—a trait Casey later confirmed was a necessary accessory for traveling from mud hole to mud hole when streams go dry.

This was a job for duct tape, so I sealed the gap, then threw in a minnow. I also tossed in a partial worm.

But the next day Fire Hydrant was gone again. I'd read in James Prosek's *Eels: An Exploration from New Zealand to the Sargasso, of the World's Most Mysterious Fish* that he tried to keep eels, but they were masters of escape that had even committed suicide by banging their heads against the glass.

I looked all over the room, and even in some adjacent rooms, but couldn't find Fire Hydrant anywhere. Still, I figured I'd keep the aquarium going, since I intended to catch an eel myself.

A couple of times, working at that desk, I thought I heard the gravel shift, but I told myself I was tripping out. I had sifted through that gravel earlier and hadn't found any traces of the eel, but two days later (or nights, rather), there she was, hanging out in the alligator grass.

Unfortunately Fire Hydrant only came out at night and wasn't letting me see her much. Some pet she turned out to be! What I was trying to observe was a creature that defied observation. No wonder Pliny and Aristotle got it wrong.

But as anyone can see on YouTube, there are plenty of eel-cams to be accessed online. You can see American eels in various stages slithering through ladders, and you can see hundreds packing the streams while ballet music suggests some sort of semi-sexual, primeval dance.

Perhaps that's what intrigued Freud—the way they swim together in spermy formation, eventually develop phallus-heads, then experience the ultimate ecstasy, recreating themselves through death. Perhaps that's why their reputation has been interpreted through a mystical lens. But whatever the case, it was time for me to get out in the field and take a more (bio)logical look.

We arrived right before sunset at the dam on the Caddo River where Casey had caught sixty eels the week before. In Arkansas yellow eels head upstream in gregarious gangs in mid-May. We were coming off a time of high activity but hoping a few stragglers were still trying to get over the dam.

Casey set up his ladder at the base of it, and I ran three hundred feet of extension cords to an outlet in the picnic area. The idea was to see if they'd be more inclined to travel through the tube if it seemed as though an alternative to the main flow provided passage beyond the obstruction. Plus, if the ladder worked, we'd catch some in the barrel.

We sat down and waited for the sun to drop. A few fishermen were casting nearby, and a guy came over.

"Whatchya fishin' for?" was the question. It turned out he was a biologist at the local Baptist college and had done his dissertation on silversides in Mexico. More important, he told us he'd seen a bunch of *Anguilla rostrata* (meaning "beaked serpent") down past the first bend.

But you have to watch out for reports like that, especially since eels are hardly seen in the light. For that matter, they're hardly ever seen in the dark either. This fellow, however, was a professional, so they might have been the real thing, or they might have been amphibians, like sirens or amphiumas. Or they might have been hallucinations, or fiction, or nothing at all—or lampreys, which are also in these waters.

I'd recently seen the lamprey episode of *River Monsters* in which Jeremy

Wade had spectacularized these creatures as "Vampires of the Deep" lurking in American waters. As usual he had solved the crime, but what I found interesting was how those literal suckers had ascended the second hugest waterfall in the United States by somehow worming their way straight up the mossy rocks while thousands of tons of hydro-pressure crashed down from above. Jeremy had gone straight into the blasting spray, groped around, and pulled them out with his hands.

Looking at that dam on the Caddo River, I wondered if eels could do the same. I'd seen videos of elvers crawling straight up concrete surfaces, so I knew they could get past certain types of barriers.

For eels, dams are both good and bad. They're problematic in the sense that they block natural movement patterns, and only a certain percentage of eels manage to get through. And dams are especially harmful when producing hydroelectricity, since a good amount of eels get ground up by turbines. On the other hand, dams help control the parasites that eels carry and spread to each other. The more dams there are in a system, the fewer parasites there are upstream. According to a 2007 USFWS report on the status of American eels, "dams and natural waterfalls, which likely preclude movement of intermediate hosts, have been shown to significantly reduce infections of eels." And at this point in time, there was a particularly powerful parasite making the rounds. In 1997 it invaded 10 to 29 percent of eel swim bladders in the Chesapeake Bay population. By 2000 more than 60 percent of Hudson Bay eels had been infected.

Dams can also cause low oxygen levels, and their construction can seriously diminish habitat availability. Along with that, the dredging that accompanies the development of dams and levees has been known to decrease distribution. Dams also cause turbidity and suspended sediments that mess with eels during all their freshwater life stages.

Other threats include overfishing, excessive harvesting of juveniles, and pathogens. Some waterways are compromised by logging or the intrusion of contaminants like heavy metals, dioxins, PCBs, and chlordane, which lower reproduction rates. Oil spills and other forms of pollution are also mentioned in various sources.

And the threats to water quality just keep coming: irrigation, water removal projects, and runoff from neighborhoods, roads, golf courses, tennis courts, etc. But the most serious threats are from changes in oceanic conditions, which can severely affect larval transport and recruitment. Since ocean currents and temperatures are driven by jet streams, and since jet streams affect the Gulf Stream, and since the Gulf Stream is now in flux due to excessive greenhouse gases, the highly delicate migration patterns of American eels are at risk of being irreversibly altered.

But it's not just eels that could suffer from the changing climatic equations. Since they're directly connected to so many species in the food chain, a shift in their balance could catastrophically impact ecosystems worldwide.

That's what Casey and I were talking about, sitting on the shore of the Caddo waiting for eels to enter the ladder. We were also talking about the world record (9.25 pounds) and the oldest one ever reported (eighty-eight years old), and the fact that eels grow larger in salt water and in the South.

When night fell we checked out the barrel (still nothing), then headed down to the boat launch to do some electrofishing. Casey had a big backpack with a motorcycle battery in it and a bunch of cords and buttons on the back. The thing probably weighed a hundred pounds. It was connected to two long-handled tools. One was an electric prong that zapped fish into temporary catatonia. The other was a net used to scoop them up.

Donning the cyborg contraption, Casey asked me to turn the main knob up to two hundred watts. Since he was wearing rubber waders, he was protected, but since I was wearing river shoes, I remained on the shore with another net, shining a spotlight into the water. If I stepped into the river while he was zapping, I'd get shocked.

Casey stepped in and started poking underneath the larger rocks. Sunfish started floating up, and then a ten-inch longnose gar. He shocked a bass, ran into a water snake, and kept heading upstream. There were lots of crawfish (a staple of larger eels), and minnows too, but no eels to be seen.

Moving upriver in the dark I was astonished by how many fish there were within just a few feet of us. You'd think they'd take off when they sensed us coming, but there were loads of species hiding out.

As the current increased, the boulders started getting larger. It was only a foot or two deep where Casey was wading, but he was encouraged by the size of the rocks.

"These are the perfect size," he told me, and then we saw an eel flash in the light and flip on its side.

Casey scooped it up and handed it to me. It was about fourteen inches long and having a seizure. For a few seconds I thought it might go into cardiac arrest, but then it shook off its daze and tried to light off.

Casey tried some more but without results. We figured that the brunt of eels from the week before had either managed to get over the dam or given up and redistributed themselves throughout the stream.

It was getting late, so we let that eel go and began packing up.

"Whatchy'all fishin' for?" a woman's voice asked, hardly audible above the rumble of her pickup truck, which sounded like a pack of Harleys.

"Eels," Casey answered, sauntering over to say hello. She was idling in the parking lot with her two teenage daughters beside her in the cab. They were texting away and seemed annoyed at their mother for talking to random strangers.

"*Eeeeels*?" she replied. "I hate those things! Caught one last week five feet long! Thick around as my arm! Whatchy'all want with those disgusting things?"

"We're collecting data," Casey said, "for U.S. Fish & Wildlife."

I went over to her window and listened in. She was in her late thirties, had a few tattoos, and wore a camo shirt with torn-off sleeves.

"It had nasty little beady eyes!" the woman continued. "How y'all fishin' for 'em?"

Casey explained the eel ladder and the zapper, but she just shook her head, acting as though we didn't know anything.

"You gotta use chicken livers!" she said, then paused for a second. "Y'all ain't fishin' for catfish, are ya?"

"Nope," Casey said, "we're not interested in those right now."

"You sure y'all ain't fishin' for catfish?" she shot back, giving him a sideways glance.

"No, no," Casey laughed, "we just want eels."

"Okay," she nodded, then propped her elbow out the window. "Y'all see that spot over there, down by the boat launch? That's the honey hole. I'm a redneck through and through, and I bring my daughters here at night, and we set up right next to the honey hole. I like river fish a whole lot more than from the store, and we catch loads of catfish in that spot! Y'all ain't gonna tell no one about the honey hole, are ya?"

"No, no," Casey assured her.

"Alright then. We catch a lot of cats in that spot. I once got one that was thirty-eight pounds. I clean 'em myself. I shoot deer too, and clean 'em as well. Anyways, last week we were trying to catch some cats, but all we kept catching was them damn eeeels! They just love chicken livers!"

At this point Casey realized she was a valuable source of information.

"Would you be willing to fill out a survey?" he asked.

She looked at him with narrowed eyes.

"It'll only take a few minutes," Casey added, "and you can mail it in."

She was not enthusiastic to respond, but Casey decided to go for it. "I'll go get it," he said, and shot off. I hadn't said anything yet, so I figured I should try to get some information.

"What kind of hooks were you using?" I asked.

"They had a one slash zero on the package . . . and they were barbless."

This didn't seem right to me, but I didn't challenge what she said. I mean, how can you make liver stay on a barbless hook? Typically, treble hooks are used for liver.

Casey came back with a survey designed for commercial fishermen and told her that it would really help him with his research. She accepted it like a pamphlet from a Jehovah's Witness, then hit the gas and drove away.

I bought a ten-dollar trotline at Walmart along with a pack of 1/0 swivel hooks and sat down to rig it up. The hooks had barbs and were small enough for a foot-long eel to get its mouth around, but I also added a few smaller hooks meant for pint-size sunfish. Those hooks were so dinky that I couldn't thread the strings through them, so instead, I used fifty-pound braided line.

It was a few days after the Caddo River, and the plan was to run the trotline beneath Remmel Dam on the Ouachita River, where Casey had caught a hundred eels two weeks before. Those eels were bigger than the Caddo eels, some of them longer than three feet.

I got off at the Malvern exit and met my assistant Scotty Lewis, who works with me on the *Toad Suck Review*. A grad student in creative writing and an avid fisherman, he was staying with his mother in Hot Springs, so only had to drive a few miles.

We found a spot downstream from the dam with tons of toaster-to microwave-sized boulders in knee-deep water. Scotty followed me upstream as I unwound the trotline, baiting it with small chunks of night crawlers. The line was 125 feet long and had twenty-five hooks dangling from it, plus a pop bottle float on each end.

I'd been trotlining hardcore for over a year, a method I found to be a massive improvement over the yo-yos I had employed for five years, fishing on Lake Conway. Yo-yos, or "auto-fishers," are spring-loaded gadgets you hang from trees. When a fish takes the bait, the spring sets the hook. I used to check my yo-yos twice a day out in the cypresses, and I frequently caught fish. But when fish are suspended, waiting for me to wake up or come home from work, they can die pretty easily—especially in warm weather, when turtles are prone to strip their flesh, leaving nothing but skeletons. Trotlines, however, keep fish underwater, where they can swish around and avoid turtles.

I'd had a lot of luck with my trotline, which is strung across a spot where a creek used to be. Catfish still travel there, as do other fish. Since I'd been running that line, I'd caught a twenty-eight-pound flathead and another that must have weighed sixty. I'd also caught crappie the size of flattened footballs, plus drum, gar, bass, bowfin, and the occasional unfortunate water bird.

Anyhow, since I'd had some practice, I felt pretty confident that I could get an eel with my custom-made small-game trotline. If they were in there, that is.

So as the sun went down, we settled into our lawn chairs and threw out some lines. A few minutes later we couldn't see our bobbers in the dark, but that didn't matter. What mattered was the trotline. And our pre-mixed gin and tonics.

An hour later the trotline floats were bopping up and down, so Scotty and I decided to check them. Now that it was darker out, we couldn't see the rocks beneath the surface, so we stumbled around like drunken clowns, removing sunfish from every other hook. If there wasn't a bluegill or rock bass on that line, the hook was usually bare.

"These dang bream are taking all our bait," I complained to Scotty, then slipped off a rock, went flailing around, and ended up falling into the river. Scotty laughed. We rebaited the line and sloshed back to shore, where we made a small fire so I could dry out.

After an hour of standing in the smoke, we figured we'd give it a final try. The trotline floats were going nuts, as they had earlier, meaning the sunfish had been raiding the buffet again. Scotty led, taking off any bait that remained and throwing back the small sunnies. I followed, winding up the line and securing the hooks. As we neared the end, I gave up entirely.

"Holy crap," Scotty said, "it's an eel."

I splashed over, and there it was, writhing and squirming and snapping at me with its razor-sharp turtlelike beak. It got me once and drew blood, but I managed to unclip the dropline and carry it back.

Meanwhile, the monster was thrashing like a spastic demon and flashing with a golden glint, tangling itself even more. It was climbing the double line and weaving in and out of it and lunging for more finger-meat. Then it began knotting itself and gnashing on the metal clip and hissing like a crazed viper.

I dropped it in my bucket and headed back to assist Scotty. We got that trotline out of there then went back to the eel, which was now way more knotted up. That fifty-pound test was wrapped around it multiple times, practically slicing into it. We had to get a knife and perform some highly surgical cuts, which was not an easy procedure. The line was actually strangling that eel, and it just kept twisting the tourniquet. I was struggling to keep my grip on it, Scotty was trying not to get chomped, and it was roaring at us like a rabid dragon. In the depths of its hellacious throat, I could see one of the smaller hooks.

It took fifteen minutes to remove the line, and I was worried about the bruises it left, now ringing its neck with stripes. Then, weasling the hook out through its gills, we beheld the behemoth sparkling with slime.

Since this was the first eel I'd caught, it meant a lot more to me than Fire Hydrant had. This leviathan was also way more freakish than the one Casey had shocked on the Caddo, no doubt due to the burbling blood spurting from its gaping maw, pumping up its creepy factor.

But the thing was . . . it was only nine inches long.

In the morning, as usual, Fire Hydrant was nowhere to be seen. Malvern, on the other hand (that's what I named her), was lying on her side in the tank, gasping as though she was suffering from organ failure—and she probably was. Getting all wound up like that had done enough damage to do her in.

I'd thrown Malvern in with Fire Hydrant, since they were both the same size, and maybe even from the same spawn. Since a female eel can produce three to forty million eggs, and since the Caddo is a tributary of the Ouachita, the possibility that they could be sisters wasn't that ridiculous.

Anyway, since it was apparent that Malvern wasn't going to make it, I tossed her into Lake Conway, where the turtles were on the prowl. I took her picture, left her there, and an hour later she was gone—another casualty for my list, wasted because I decided to play God. Or biologist.

FIG. 1. Malvern the American eel. Photo by Scotty Lewis.

Or fish writer—who believes he has to capture a creature in order to know it better, consequences be damned!

The next day I drove Fire Hydrant to the Arkansas River and let her go. She was a crummy pet anyhow, very unsocial and never around. Observing her was like trying to keep a phantom locked up.

But I hesitate to employ this experience as a metaphor, because that's too obvious. Malvern was an isolated case. Still, when something like this happens, it's in our nature to try to place it into perspective. It's also in our nature to moralize—which is what I'm trying to avoid right now. So let's look at the facts instead:

In 2004 the USFWS received a petition to protect the American eel under the Endangered Species Act. After three years of research and debate, scientists decided there wasn't enough evidence to prove that extinction was an imminent threat.

This assessment, however, was challenged in 2011 when the USFWS responded to another petition, in light of the fact that the 2007 status review hadn't thoroughly assessed population structure, the impact of the parasitic nematode *Anguillicola crassus*, declining long-term glass eel recruitment numbers, and the effects of global warming.

So essentially we're still hashing out the details of the 2007 ruling. And since hashing out details requires data, that's where Casey and others come in—in regions where virtually nothing is known about eel movement patterns, distribution, or how to make an effective ladder.

Understandably, we have a lot more historical data on American eels from the East than from the West. We've been watching eels longer and more closely in the East, where they're more established as part of the fishery culture. Hence, it's the research from the East, I suspect, that will determine the overall status of the American eel.

I also suspect that because this fish's disposition has already been evaluated in excruciating detail, it's doubtful that new federal studies will be funded unless it's absolutely essential. This attitude echoes our tendency in human nature not to treat a wound until it's infected, when prevention would have been the more pragmatic choice in the first place.

Still, that's easy to say, sitting in my shed, typing on my laptop, staring out at the world in the way I perceive it. I know I'm idealistic; I know eels are gradually going down; and I know it's ridiculous to claim we should have thought more about the effects of climate change before allowing the petrochemical industries to confuse scientific fact with strategic disinformation and denial.

Nope, it's too late for prevention. And it's also too late for the European eel, which has experienced a 99 percent population loss due to industry, development, pollution, dams, the whole enchilada. An enchilada we are eating now: the range of the American eel is down to 75 percent of what it used to be in the nation's watersheds.

But if there's one saving grace for the American eel, it's that the species is able to endure a wide range of environmental conditions. According to the USFWS, eels "have the broadest diversity of habitats of any fish species in the world." This means they're capable of surviving *here* if eliminated *there*, since they're all one population, spawning in the same spot. Additionally, eels are able to withstand all sorts of temperature and salinity levels, which accounts for how they survived several ice ages.

My highly biased conclusion, then, is that this baffling and bizarre fish will continue its slippery legacy as long as there's a Sargasso Sea. And even if this species crashes, eels will persevere in our imaginations (assuming we can outlast them) as they've done for millennia.

Realistically, though, imaginary fish are a poor substitute for the real thing.

2

Environmental Lemonade

Dealing with the Creature That
Put the "Ish" in "Fish"

They're eely, they're mucousy, they've got huge salamander-looking heads with bulging bubble eyes, and they're devouring the lake trout, rainbow trout, cutthroats, Kokanee salmon, smallmouth bass, and almost everything else in Flaming Gorge—a sprawling, snaking, sixty-six-square-mile reservoir on the Wyoming-Utah border. The fear, of course, is that this invader from the North will lay waste to the Green River ecosystem.

Illegally introduced in the early nineties, burbot have been bumming out anglers, state agencies, and chambers of commerce for decades. The habitat of this cold, deep body of water offers optimum conditions for this opportunistic fish. The rubbly scree slopes provide tons of crayfish and bass to feed on as well as places for burbot fry to hide, and the silty, sandy tributaries are ideal for spawning. With adult females releasing between half a million and three million eggs per spawn, this truly grotesque freshwater cod has become, in essence, a uniquely grotesque terrorist.

That's why there's a Burbot Bash. It happens every year and there are two main parts. The first tournament occurs in November, and the fishing is done from boats. The second tournament happens in January on the ice. This fishing pressure helps control the exploding numbers of this invasive species. The contests remove thousands every year, and the attention attracts anglers throughout the year, who remove thousands more. Putting these serpentine slimers back in is against the law, but luckily for us, they're damn tasty.

Known as lawyer, ling, loche, lush, cusk, maria, wethy, spineless catfish, gudgeon, mud blower, and a host of other regional names, the burbot (*Lota lota*) finds the root of its name in the Latin word *barba*, meaning beard, due to its single wormy barbel beneath the chin. It is commonly known as an eelpout in quite a few places. Calling this camo-colored fish an eelpout, however, is misleading. Sure, they might look like a cross between an eel and a bullhead (or "horned pout" as they're called in New England), but the true eelpouts are from the Zoarcidae family, of which there are more than 220 species. The burbot is in the Gadidae family.

And they're all over the world. They're in Europe, Asia, Russia, Canada, and just about every northern country on the planet with latitudes right beneath the Arctic Circle. In the United States they are distributed from Washington to Maine, with their southernmost populations dipping down into Missouri and Utah. Which is why I found myself starting my sabbatical by winding through a great ancient canyonland of scrubby brush and beautiful buttes. There were antelope everywhere and snow-dusted mesas busting up from the winter crust. I saw herds of elk, migrations of deer, three coyotes, and plenty of golden eagles, and I knew I was back in a place that was part of me, from which I'd been absent for too many years. This geologically dramatic landscape—stratified by layers of red, orange, purple and gold—always kicks me square in the heart. I don't know if this effect is due to the terrain feeling familiar or alien, but I know it's spectacular, and it never fails to choke me up.

I was heading to the 2014 Burbot Bash in Manila, Utah, to investigate a creature celebrated for its grodiness, and I was also tackling a personal demon head on. I come from Minnesota, but I've never liked—or understood—the concept of ice fishing. I was prepared, though, with hundreds of dollars of high-tech long underwear, an extreme-weather winter jacket, padded pants good to thirty below, super-warm boots, and specialized gloves. Brian Raymond of the Manila Chamber of Commerce knew I was coming to cover the three-day event, and I was hoping he could hook me up with a local burbot-bashing team. I had two goals. One: to get the story. And two: to catch myself a burbot.

Awaking at the Villa Inn on Friday morning, I went to the local hardware store, where I bought a two-foot-long ice-fishing rod, a peen scoop, a package of sucker meat, some glow-in-the-dark jigs, and a Wyoming fishing permit to piggyback on my Utah license. After that I headed over to the Villa Restaurant, where I had biscuits and gravy for breakfast, then met with the Daggett County commissioners. They were registering fishermen, which meant handing out information packets and talking about safety on the ice. All anglers were told to bring ropes and ice picks, and if driving four-wheelers or snowmobiles on the ice, they had to wear life jackets.

With my homemade "PRESS" badge, I hovered in the shadows taking notes. The year before, more than fourteen hundred burbot bashers in the contest had removed over four thousand burbot from the lake. This year there were fewer contestants but over $100,000 in prizes, including raffles. And if you caught a fish with a tag, the bounties ranged from $200 to $25,000.

It had been controversial catching burbot, then tagging them and putting them back to breed. The logic, however, was that the tags lured fishermen, and the fishermen, in turn, removed more burbot than Wyoming Game and Fish and the Utah Department of Wildlife Resources could do together with trammel nets. In a sense, these states had been handed a bunch of lemons, so now they were making lemonade.

Whereas most global populations of burbot are either stable or in decline, this population had been growing for years. But from the billions of eggs jettisoned every winter, only a fraction are ever successfully fertilized. After that, only thousands survive to become adults. Hundreds of humans then come along and remove thousands of burbot from the lake.

The hope is that this process will eventually lead to more manageable numbers, and that seems to be what's happening.

I began talking to the anglers, trying to gauge how they felt about this fish. From what I gathered, it was a love-hate relationship. The citizens in this area love their trout and the tourism that comes from trout, but they also love the tourism that comes from burbot. Though most locals professed to hate this fish, a burbot-focused culture had nevertheless established itself as a novelty in the region—with the potential, perhaps, to become even more popular than trout. But if they let that happen, then a longer-standing part of their identities would be lost to a new wave of introduced species devouring an old guard of introduced species.

As non-native species ourselves, in most places where we exist, we tend to prefer species we've come to perceive as "natural resources," even if they aren't. Lake trout, after all, are landlocked salmon. They used to rule Flaming Gorge, but now the new top predators on the block are burbot, which not only compete with trout for food but swallow whole trout half their size.

Anyway, I was eager to get out in the field. But since I didn't have an auger, I needed someone to aug for me. I told this to the Daggett County commissioners, and they assured me that if I walked out on the ice and started talking to anglers, someone would eventually drill me a hole. Someone also told me that if I headed north to Road 11, then turned right and went to the end, my chances would be good that I'd catch a burbot.

So that's what I did.

All mummied up, I trekked out into the wind with my PRESS tag hanging from my jacket. I had my gear in a five-gallon bucket, and I could see that the ice was a foot thick. It warbled as I walked, sending out weird burbling sounds and distant cracks that made me flinch. But as I could see, there were others on the ice, and they weren't running from the swelling, swaling undulations beneath the frozen skin.

FIG. 2. Two three-foot burbots. Photo by Mark Spitzer.

I approached a spot in the middle, a scattering of ice holes surrounded by canvas chairs and gear. The only person out there was a teenage boy who had a couple of lake trout lying on the ice. I introduced myself as "the Press" and talked with him for a bit. He wasn't catching burbot, though, and he didn't offer to auger me a hole, so I moved on to the next spot—sometimes stopping, wondering if I should just give up.

It felt forced to operate this way. To get a hole, I had to chat someone up, which just wasn't me. But since I had just driven thirteen hundred miles, and since it would be lame to wuss out, I wasn't me either. So the me I wasn't approached two guys who'd staked out another spot. I told them I was here to get the story.

"The story on what?"

"The story on burbot."

"You bet, brother!" the burlier guy replied, and pointed to two three-footers lying on the snow, occasionally flopping around. They were about seven pounds each, which is pretty big for this fishery. The world record, however, is twenty-five pounds. That fish came from Saskatchewan. They don't get much longer than four feet.

We talked for a bit, and then I got what I came out for.

"Want me to drill you a hole, buddy?"

"Awesome!" I told him, and he broke out a gas-powered auger.

A minute later I was sitting on my bucket and jigging a chunk of sucker meat off the bottom, which was fifty-something feet below. We knew this because they had a portable fish finder, and they were watching for activity.

The older guy showed me the tackle he caught his two burbots on (a big silver-blue spoon tipped with a hunk of sucker meat), then started ribbing his friend about not catching anything. They bantered with each other and joked around as I hung out listening to them sounding a lot like what I jokingly call my "Fishing Support Group" in Arkansas.

Then BONK! it hit, just like I'd seen on the short video *Burbot Fishing* on YouTube. An underwater camera was focused on a "spawning ball," because that's what burbot do: they get together in a writhing mass of ten or fifteen fish, and if you doink a jig up and down in the middle of a swarm, they strike like big fat dummies that don't even fight. Burbot after burbot, they just kept getting hooked and hauled to the surface. My favorite part was at the four-minute mark when two burbot struck one jig at once, and both got yanked up.

Yep, it had to be a burbot on my line, because it was coming up like a log. My $24.99 rod was bending to the max, and I had to tighten the drag. But when it became visible, I saw that it was just a lake trout.

"Aww man!" I complained. "It's just a garbage fish!"

It was a three-pounder, a beautiful fish, but it wasn't what I'd come to get. Still, it was food, and since I'd never caught one before, I kept it as my companions took off for another spot. I then jigged for another half hour, but nothing was biting, so I gave up.

That night I put on more layers and went out again, this time to a spot known as the Confluence (of the Green and Blacks Fork rivers), where I decided to try my luck again. The word on the street was that burbot were out deeper during the day, but at dusk they moved into six to ten feet of water, and that's where they were caught all night—which is the best time to fish for them.

I parked down at Lost Dog then headed out on the creaking ice. It was creepy being out in the blackness wondering if I might fall through, but the Milky Way was out in sparkling force, lending a supernatural shimmer to the strong, crisp bite of the sky.

With my Scotch-taped laser-printed PRESS badge, I approached several outposts on the far side of the lake, where tents were set up, most of them surrounded by ATVs and propane tanks. There was camouflage everywhere, and snowmobiles and sleds full of gear. With my official-looking homemade badge, I must have looked like a game warden walking up to check people out, but when they found out I was there to get the story, they were always glad to show me their burbot.

The first guy I met introduced himself as Robert and offered to drill me a hole. I thanked him and told him I'd be back after I checked with others in the area. Nobody was catching much, but everyone was glad to talk burbot. People were friendly, interested, and glad to be freezing their asses off, and no one was getting super-drunk.

Sure, some were enjoying a drink or two, but the overall atmosphere was totally opposite of what I imagined to be the case with the other famous burbot event: the annual Eelpout Festival in Walker, Minnesota, a town of fifteen hundred that mushrooms to ten times that size every February. Their festival on Leech Lake features a burbot curling competition (they're frozen in blocks of ice and their tails act as handles), burbot rugby, and a "Pout Plunge" in which hundreds of daring Nordic types leap into nut-freezing openings cut in the ice. Though some go there to fish for burbot, it seems that most go there to party till they puke. In 2013 the *Brainerd Dispatch* quoted Commissioner Jim Dowson, who claimed that 95 percent of the participants are intoxicated. I basically confirmed this by watching a YouTube video that shows hot women in cold parkas strip-teasing down to bikinis while tons of drunken dudes howl like frat boys at a wet t-shirt contest. The *Brainerd Dispatch* also notes that there's a problem with tons of "trash, garbage, and human waste" being left on the ice after the event is over, and the Cass County Sherriff is frustrated at the crime and debauchery.

But out at Flaming Gorge I saw a lot of families. Parents brought their kids, husbands brought their wives. They were camping in trailers on the shore and tents on the ice, with barbecues and picnic tables set up all over the place. People were walking around visiting one another's camps, and there was definitely a social feel in the frigid air.

Eventually I wandered back to Robert's camp and he drilled me a hole. So I baited up, focused my light on my glow-jig, then dropped it in. We talked about his job as a specialized Air Force technician, and we talked about mine as a creative writing professor. His wife drank a Budweiser Clamato Chelada and reclined in a lawn chair, and again I was grateful that strangers would take me in and be so welcoming.

But sitting there—jigging, jigging, jigging and not catching anything—I began to recall why I disliked ice fishing. There's just something about this kind of below-freezing-just-sitting-there-non-action that makes me lose patience. Maybe it's the lack of actual movement or not being able to see much, but whatever the case, after an hour I got tired of staring into an indifferent hole, so I gave up again.

The next day the check-in began at the Buckboard Marina, one of the three check-in locations. I met the officials there at eight o'clock in the morning, and with my trusty PRESS badge I was able to position myself right in the middle of the action. Working with Wyoming Game and Fish, I counted the burbot as they came in by the cooler-load. They were transferred to tubs, counted, and scanned for micro-sized PIT (passive integrated transponder) tags embedded in the abdomen, then measured if they had a chance of placing for largest or smallest fish. The two- to four-member teams could either donate their catches to the upcoming fish fry or keep the fish for themselves—but they had to chop off the tails of any they kept so that these couldn't be reused by other contestants.

The first team, Slaugh, brought in twenty-one burbot, and the second team, Team Tuna, brought in eighty-one, including a 35.5-incher that weighed 7.4 pounds. After that a team called Straightline brought in eight, the Four J's brought in six, That's Right brought in eight, Walleye36 brought in nineteen, the Iceholes brought in ten, Chuck's Burbot Camp came in with three, the Thollman Trollers had two, Olson44 dumped eight in a tub, and Team Gas yielded three. For the most part, it had been a slow night.

Hook Line and Sinker then came in with sixty-eight, including a tagged fish and a 9.5-incher which was a good contender for the smallest burbot. Millstream came in with twenty-six, the Bourbon Bots brought in nine, the Cavemen ten, the Diggs twenty-eight, Team Climax had five, Team Iceholes (not to be confused with *the* Iceholes) had fourteen, and Bent Rod brought in twenty-four, including a 7.67-pound fatty, which was heavier than Team Tuna's big one. Length, however, was what counted in this contest—but weight could be a tie-breaker.

Next, Ray Lynn Dawn brought in twenty-six burbot, and the Arizona Ice Anglers came in with twelve, including the second tagged fish of the day. I could go into the other numbers caught, but what's more interesting are the team names. Ie, Fish Corps, Ling Kings, Team Slime, the Badass Burbot Bashers, Any Hour, Kiss Our Bur-Butts, Team Shoepick [*sic*], and the Wild Turkeys (they had ninety fish, two with tags). I had hoped to meet A Cop, a Fat Guy, and a Little Girl, but they never showed up at my check-in station. Nor did the Burbounators, Spawners, Auger Floggers, Team Donkey Bomber, BassTards, Dingalings, or Harley Hillbillies.

Meanwhile down in Manila it was reported that a team had brought in 167 burbot. Overall, at least two thousand burbot were culled from the lake that day by 401 participants.

And it was good to work with Wyoming Game and Fish. Fisheries Supervisor Robert Keith was glad to respond to questions regarding sustainability. He felt that they were "over the hump" in terms of thinning the Flaming Gorge burbot populations, but they still had a lot of work to do. He also had some good information on the illegal introduction of burbot into the system. He figured somebody brought them over the Continental Divide, then intentionally dumped them at different spots. The ages and sizes of the oldest fish they'd caught had matched up, which suggests that they were introduced at the same time.

Then, at 11:00 a.m., the check-in was over, and the Game and Fish agents began bagging some for themselves. "Some mercury to take home for the kids," one agent joked, then asked me if I'd like some as well. I threw four in a garbage bag and went back to my motel room.

I could've gone back out on the ice that afternoon, but the wind was blowing hard, and frankly, I just didn't feel like putting all those layers back on—especially when the consensus was that the burbot just weren't biting like the year before. Which could mean that the year-round harvesting was taking its toll. Or it could mean that they just weren't biting.

I decided to try the Utah side of the reservoir, which was extremely different from the Wyoming side. Whereas the Wyoming side was frozen and cold, the Utah end had open water, and Sheep Creek Cove was sheltered from the wind. With the sun beating down, and all those bright colors blazing away across the bay, it was warm enough to sit there in my shirt sleeves trying to convince myself that I wasn't slacking off. Nope, I was doing serious research!

Still, I knew that burbot spawn under the ice. With the spawn on, they were no doubt at the other end of the lake.

So actually, I was slacking off. Yep, I was kicking back in the sun, watching the loons and coots tool by, and I had my ice-fishing rod baited up with a crayfish. Nothing was biting, but I didn't care.

I was reflecting. First on the thought that if the catch was low out on the lake, maybe this meant that the burbot being caught were getting ready to move into the tributaries. I'd read in a few places that it's mostly the males that group together in the spawning balls, which led me to wonder where the females were. Could they be upstream in the rivers waiting for their guys? Maybe. But then again, I'd talked to a few fishermen who'd been fishing on the rivers. Some had done well, some got skunked. Whatever the case, I figured I'd shoot up to the Green River arm that evening and take a look.

But I was also reflecting on what burbot ate. According to Rob Buffler and Tom Dickson in *Fishing for Buffalo,* "Frogs . . . Q-tips, cigarettes, suckers, carp, mollusks, mice, burbot, crappies, rockbass, smallmouth bass, sculpin, smelt, crustaceans, minnows, shrews, perch, cisco, sunfish, insects, invertebrates, fish eggs, rocks, wood chips, and plastic pieces" have been found in burbot. An hour before, though, I'd cleaned my burbot in my motel bathtub, filleting them on the toilet tank cover. When I cut into them, I found them packed full of fresh crayfish—which is where I got the slightly unorthodox bait on my line.

This reflection led to another reflection—on the figure of "544 metric tons of crayfish," which was the amount of crayfish Dr. Chris Lueke from Utah State University estimated the peak upper-population of burbot in this reservoir consumed in 2011. That population had been pegged at 289,000, which, according to a study entitled "Burbot Summary 2011," meant that the 4,022 burbots caught in the Burbot Bash that year represented "1.4% of the burbot fishery." Those burbot devoured "122 metric tons of fish, and 11 metric tons of 'other' invertebrates on an annual basis."

A fishery biologist from Wyoming Game and Fish told me that diet studies had been conducted on adjoining waterways, and they found that different burbot populations consumed different amounts of different stuff. It depended, of course, on what was in those other systems, and what sort of competition those other bodies of water experienced. In some of the neighboring systems there were walleye, so there were different dynamics going on. In some cases the walleye were beating out the burbot, and in others it was vice versa. Wyoming Game and Fish is currently partnering with the Utah Division of Wildlife Resources on annual netting, and they're collecting data in order to know more.

I didn't get a bite that afternoon, and with a lazy attitude like that, it was looking doubtful that I'd catch myself a burbot. I began to worry that catching a burbot was not destined to be part of this story.

On Sunday morning there was one main check-in at the city park in Manila, presided over by Utah wildlife officials. Out of the 2,927 burbot caught on Saturday, 1,500 had been filleted, so no more were needed for the fish fry. According to the woman who oversaw that operation, the filleting team had been made up of "four dehiders and four filleters," and they'd worked all night.

Biology students from Western Wyoming Community College were also on hand to collect specimens for research. I talked to their professor, Dr. Will Clark, who told me they were doing studies on diet analysis, reproduction, and growth rates. He also said that they were looking for parasites like tapeworms and river flukes, which are only present in about 10 percent.

Since Will was a burbot biologist, I told him about my hypothesis—that if the males were out in the lake, then maybe the females were in the rivers. I had tried to investigate this by going up to Green River the night before to check out the fishing. The four-wheel-drive trail kept getting rougher and rougher, and since there were no recent tire tracks on the snow, I figured that nobody was risking fishing where I was heading, which was starting to look like Stucksville. That's why I turned back.

Will replied that burbot tend to spawn in the mouths of rivers, and that if they do go upstream, they're probably following baitfish. My theory was then further dismantled when I checked back with the woman who'd overseen the burbot cleaning. She told me that there were just as many females full of eggs as males full of milt, and since most of these fish were caught in the reservoir, my hypothesis was shot.

Then the fish began flowing in. Slime Slime Slime Slime! The slimiest fish I ever saw! Pools of snotty oozy gooby goo congealing in the bottoms of coolers, glooping from bags, yucky buckets overflowing,

FIG. 3. A tournament participant. Photo by Mark Spitzer.

pungent mucous everywhere! If anything was grotesque about this fish, it was this.

Team Stapp brought in twenty, Walleye36 had six, Hooked on Fishing claimed twenty-six, and Tip Up came in with eight. Reel Action removed seventeen, Boone Outdoors had eleven, Olson44 had four, Redneck had thirteen, and That's Right brought in nine. J.J. Jiggers, the Linguinis, Ramrod, Brigg's Construction, the Burbot Killers, Johnny P's Fish Killers, and the Iceholes accounted for 117 total.

A team called Asay then pumped up the expectations, bringing in sixty-eight, one of which was tagged. The teams that followed included TNB, Just for Fun, Stinkbait, Team Iceholes II, the Diggs, the Clam, and Shoepick—who brought in the smallest burbot thus far: 9.3 inches. These teams were responsible for subtracting 145 burbot from the reservoir.

Then came Straightline with eighteen, Bamf with eight, KKA with four, Tempton with seven, Team Climax with eleven, and the big-money team Schofield with 124, including two tagged burbot. After that, teams George, Slime, Knight, Eduardo and the Three Hocos, the Cowboys, Ice Shanty Utah, Ted York, Fish Corps, Tuna, the Burbot Slayers, Hardcore Hookers, Burbot Bashers, Blair, and Advantage Oilfield Services accounted for 225.

The biology students stopped collecting specimens at about five hundred. Most burbots after that began piling up in the dumpster.

The next teams to come in were the First Timers, Willard, the Ling-Slingers, Hook Line and Sinker, Reel Crazy Fishermen, and Addicted to Fishing (they had sixty-one). Daddy Daughter Burbot Bashers, Team Intrepid, the Thollman Trollers, the Cavemen, Team Gas, Millstream, and the Lip Rippers (they had forty-nine) came in next. Any Hour, and my favorite team, the Wild Turkeys (with seventy), then weighed in. These teams brought in 266 total.

As the morning went on, the Ling Kings ambled in, followed by Team Mandy, Bent Rod, Mandy Mae, the Arizona Ice Anglers, the Eelpout Devastators, Team Icehole, the other Team Icehole, Robert Blake (not the actor), Slagowski JJ, 302, and Wild Turkey (the singular team, as opposed to the plural one). These teams removed 174 from the lake.

Then suddenly the check-in was over. A grand total of 4,039 burbots had been taken out of Flaming Gorge Reservoir.

The filleting contest was already going, so I made my way over there. This competition was open to contest participants only. They went head to head, three at a time, while families and friends and fishermen watched from the bleachers. It was a complicated procedure. You cut a ring around their necks, peel off the skin with pliers (in one stroke, preferably), make some special cuts to take out the eely dorsal, then cut along the ribs somehow. There are online videos demonstrating the proper technique, which I bypassed in my motel room the day before, opting for a vertical cut behind the gills followed by one clean slice down the spine on both sides, then skinning off the skin (which looks like catfish skin, but their slick hides are covered in tiny trout-like scales). I missed some meat along the edges with this primitive method, but I got eight good slaps of burbot off four fish, and I'm not bothered by the bones.

The filleting contest was judged for technique and least amount of waste. There was a five-minute time limit as well, but I didn't stick around to see the results, because I wanted to check out the dumpster.

It was full of hundreds of burbots, most with their tails cut off. One burbot, however, caught my eye. It was a fourteen-incher, its tail was still intact, its color hadn't faded yet, and its clear eyes hadn't sunk into its head.

An evil thought crossed my mind: *I could take that burbot and revive it.* After all, I'd talked to beaucoup fishermen who claimed you just couldn't kill 'em. One guy said that he cut one's stomach open and left it on the ice where it thrashed around for two hours. Others claimed the same thing for burbot tossed on the snow. I hadn't seen any literature on burbot having air-breathing organs similar to bowfin or snakeheads (both of which the burbot resembles), but I'd seen burbot flopping on the ice, staying alive while lake trout died.

So I snuck that burbot back to my Jeep. I had no idea what I was going to do with it, but I knew it wasn't quite legal to be taking this fish. Still, wildlife agents from Wyoming and Utah had seen thousands of live burbot brought in for this contest, and some had taken some breathers home.

I drove to Sheep Creek and got some water in my bucket, then put the burbot in the bucket. I thought I saw it gasp, but I couldn't be sure. Then I took it back to my motel, filled the sink with creek water, and put the burbot in the sink, where it could have more room to stretch out. I set up an aerator I'd brought along, then covered the whole thing with a life jacket in case it tried to leap out.

If anything, I was conducting an experiment. If it lived, I'd put it in a tank, and then I'd have a new grotesque to observe. If it died, then I'd have a better idea about what they can take. Either way, I figured I'd show it to my father in New Mexico on my way back to Arkansas. But since the closing ceremonies were about to begin, I skedaddled back to the festival.

That's when things became as wiggly as a burbot barbel, though they might've been that way all along. In the last two days three teams had gone through the ice. The first was a couple of good ol' boys on an ATV. They'd been tearing across the lake at night and had hit an open hole. The next thing they knew, the tires were keeping the vehicle afloat while they swam around in the freezing water tying on a rope. Some other fishermen helped out, and they managed to pull it out. The team next to me at the motel had also gone through the ice. They had two snowmobiles pulling two sleds full of gear, and they'd hit a soft spot the night before. They had to hang their stuff up to dry and had given up on the contest. The other team had been on a four-wheeler, a man and his wife. They hit a hole in the middle of the night, and the wife called out for help. Some nearby fishermen came rushing with ropes and pulled them out. It was a pretty close call, with the husband physically paralyzed and the wife mentally paralyzed, so I heard.

It surprised me that no one had died or gone into hypothermia, and it surprised me that taking such risks to catch burbot was par for the course. In Minnesota, where I'm from, only fools risked going out on thin ice and ripping around in the night.

So there was an element of danger out there, and there was definitely a tension at the contest, which was being emceed by a local television host. When I was standing in front of him with a photographer who was also shooting the awards, I became a bit miffed at the record keeping. The day before, Wyoming officials had miscounted a team's catch and recorded an incorrect number, which I strove to correct. But now that TV clown was telling the audience that four thousand burbot had been caught, and since they lay six million eggs each, this meant that twenty-four billion burbot had been prevented from coming into existence—which was wrong! First of all, not all those burbot were egg-bearing females. Second, six million eggs was way off. And third, the survival rate isn't that high.

I kept my mouth shut, though. Until, that is, he announced the winner for the smallest burbot, a 9.5-incher. Knowing that the smallest burbot was 9.3 inches, I walked over and told him. He seemed confused, but some other fishermen backed me up. That award was worth six hundred bucks.

I should mention that a number of raffle prizes had already been awarded, including a two-year lease on a brand new Ford F-150, an eight-hundred-dollar fly rod (one guy won both), a .22 rifle, and a good number of gift certificates from local businesses. During that time Mr. TV Personality also announced that the fourteen tagged fish caught in the contest hadn't been tagged by Daggett County and were therefore worthless.

Then came the award for the most burbot, which went to Team Schofield. They caught 202, which earned them $2,500. This was followed by the award for the largest burbot, in which the TV guy rattled off a figure I found myself disputing in front of hundreds in the audience—and he was not pleased.

In an aside to me, he growled that *his figures* were the official results, mine were not official, and I was undermining the entire contest. Nevertheless, I expected accuracy and that the anglers should get credit for what they caught, but to that fellow I was an invasive species with a PRESS tag stepping out of my objective role.

So I stepped over to the frying area where burbot fillets were being handed out for free. The meat was sweet and the cornmeal crust had a spicy kick. It was excellent fish!

Back in my motel room, however, the burbot in my sink had gone belly up.

I never caught a burbot with rod and reel, but I did get the story. The story is I went to the Burbot Bash, I tried to accept ice fishing and failed, and I saw a lot of slimy fish. In the end I got my burbot in a questionable manner and stopped by my father's place and cooked up a pot of "poor man's lobster" with the fillets from the motel room.

Most recipes I'd seen said to boil sugared water, then throw in some burbot chunks for five to seven minutes. One recipe, though, said to boil the fish in 7-Up. I was intrigued by the soda pop route, so that's what I did. We then dipped the meat in melted butter with garlic salt, and incredibly, it tasted a hell of a lot like lobster. My conclusion was that these fast-growing, delicious fish could make for an excellent commercial fishery. They can be harvested from the wild where they're not wanted, or maybe they can be farmed en masse. Someone should definitely look into this.

The lesson from the burbot in my sink might be that they're not as tough as we think they are. Maybe they've got some chinks in their armor we haven't yet discovered. There's still a lot of research to be done. But if we find the means to eliminate them from the Flaming Gorge system, it might be a mistake to take them all out—because they're definitely worth introducing to our taste buds.

FIG. 4. Taxidermy by Best of Birds, Conway, Arkansas. Photo by Mark Spitzer.

POSTSCRIPT

When I got back to Arkansas I took that burbot to my local taxidermist. He'd never seen anything like it in his life and told me it would be hard to mount since there are no premade forms for this fish. He told me he'd have to carve one from wood, but if I wanted him to try, he'd take a shot.

Looking down at that fat-bellied, bubble-eyed burbot with its single slimy barbel, I answered, "Well, since you can't make it any uglier than it already is . . . let's go for it."

3

Urban Sturgeon

A Totally Unique Fishery in Portland, Oregon

Last time I fished with Bartek, I caught a four-foot sturgeon on the Willamette River. We put it on a stringer, and that's when the earthquake hit. The epicenter was up in Olympia, and it shook the rock I was standing on in Portland. Joggers on the walking path stopped and we looked at one another with confused expressions as flowerpots fell from apartment balconies. The sturgeon, however, didn't flinch, and after that, they just wouldn't bite.

That was twelve years ago, but now I'm back again, fishing on the same waterway with Lars Larsen and Bartek Prusiewicz. Lars is my jolly, joking filmmaking buddy from back in Bohemian France, and burly Bartek is his sculptor pal who doubles as a sturgeon whisperer. He's been sturgeoning this river for years as well as the Columbia River Gorge.

It's the beginning of March and rainy as hell. We're on the edge of a concrete dock at the end of the biking/running/skateboarding path winding through downtown. The condos peter out at this point and all there is downstream are ghostly factories and abandoned warehouses. There's construction going on behind us, but the dock is open to anyone who drives down the sidewalk, then baits up and casts out—which might not last very long. Bartek says there's a dispute about who owns this property with nothing on it except a giant yellow public arts sculpture and Lars's orange and white VW van, where we're waiting for the dark gray thunderheads to stop rumbling down from the ferny, mossy mountains above.

Across the Willamette, barges are moored beneath a clanking railroad yard. There's a homeless camp halfway up the opposite bank and a classic bald eagle perched in a tree. The setting isn't pretty, but so what? I've always loved fishing in places like this, which I like to think of as "the Industrial Edge." As a college student in Minneapolis, my favorite place to fish wasn't up in the Boundary Waters, or on the forested shores of a pristine lake, or along any crumbling limestone bluff—it was at the University of Minnesota power plant near downtown. There was a rushing interstate bridge above (the one that collapsed in 2007, killing seven people), a lock and dam to one side and on the other a crazy metallic Frank Ghery museum that catches the sunset at dusk and reflects it back like a futuristic space station. At night the lights of the city merge with the stars and you never know what sort of one-eyed monster you'll haul from the roiling depths.

There's just something to say about places where the city meets the wilderness. These ecotones of smokestacks and cinderblocks and rusty pipes and climbing ivies are alive with a vivid tension that you don't experience when you're in a vast, managed national forest or a carefully manicured park. Plus these places are always easy to get to, and they don't involve packing a whole lot of specialized gear. You just throw your stuff in your car, grab a six pack, wind your way through the hobos and roadkill, and there you are: a creature in a place where extremes converge. And the fish there, they're just like you—in the sense that they also exist at the crossroads of industry and the natural world.

Such settings make monsters seem even more monstrous—which is why Godzilla rampaged through Tokyo. I mean, no one would have cared if he took a stroll through some isolated woods. But knocking down skyscrapers and getting tangled in the power grid, that's the stuff of pure Jungian psycho-terror. Such nightmares illustrate the clash between our "primitive" and "civilized" selves, a dynamic as old as literature itself; the wild man Enkidu in the *Epic of Gilgamesh*, circa 2000 BC, embodied such a fusion.

So when the rain lets up, we emerge from the van, envisioning municipal monsters lurking on the edge of the wild.

The number one question regarding sturgeon is: How big do they get? Here's my answer to that. There are twenty-seven known species of sturgeon in the world, of which the beluga and kaluga are the largest. In 1736 a whopping twenty-eight-foot beluga weighing 4,570 pounds was caught in Russia at the mouth of the Volga. In the United States the official record is only 486 pounds. That nine-foot, six-inch fish was caught in California by Joey Pallotta in 1983. It was a white sturgeon (otherwise known as Pacific, Oregon, California, Columbia or Sacramento sturgeon), which is the largest freshwater fish in North America. Larger white sturgeon have been caught—like the twelve-foot, four-inch 1,100-pounder caught in the Fraser River in British Columbia in 2012, but the weight of that fish, was unofficial because you can't legally weigh those old-school, oversized sturgeon anymore. It's against the law to take them out of the water, so you have to use a chart to determine their weight based on length. Then, because of this fish's sensitive status, catch and release is required.

Meanwhile, numerous fish books and websites note the mythical length of twenty feet being the white sturgeon's max, even though there's no official record of one ever being this long. Fourteen- and fifteen-footers have been caught in the twentieth century, and a one-ton monster from the Columbia River was stuffed and exhibited at the 1893 World's Fair in Chicago, but there are no records of its length. It's possible that there might be an eighteen-footer swimming around somewhere out there, no doubt well over a century old, but after 5.5 million pounds of sturgeon were commercially harvested from the Columbia River in 1892, we haven't seen many surpassing the twelve-foot mark.

Sturgeon are anadromous, meaning that they spawn in fresh water and can live in both salt and fresh water. The white sturgeon ranges along the West Coast from Monterey to Alaska Bay. They enter only a few rivers, and there are different concerns for different populations. For example, when hydroelectric dams and irrigation facilities were constructed in the twentieth century, especially on the Columbia and Snake rivers, eighteen subpopulations became landlocked. These dams also messed with the bottom, causing sediment to build up, which isn't conducive to the rocky substrate sturgeon require for reproduction. The Kootenai River in Idaho and Montana (which is as far as white sturgeon range to the east) is a good example of a population that can't spawn anymore. Those sturgeon are listed as endangered species, and their numbers are in rapid decline. By 2030, they'll be extinct.

The Willamette population is considered healthy and sustainable. In this tributary of the lower Columbia, these sturgeon can still find the right bottom to broadcast their eggs, and they can go out to the ocean whenever they want. But that's not to say this population isn't threatened. Aggressive sea lions are a factor, and these days, they're traveling farther up the system, devouring sturgeon as they go. And, of course, there's the constant toxic demon of pollution and insecticides taking a toll on sturgeon.

Hence wherever white sturgeon are, there are limits on how many you can take. On the Willamette, you can take one sturgeon per day between thirty-eight and fifty-four inches, but this year, the local quota has already been reached for these waters, and some fishermen are mad about that. Still, it's strict fishery management tactics like this that are preserving diverse populations and bringing numbers back up.

As a commercial fish, sturgeon are valued mostly for their roe. Richard Adams Carey's book *The Philosopher Fish* does an excellent job at examining the international caviar trade—both legal and black market—and the politics that have resulted from this commerce. A lot of poaching continues to go on. In fact, there are YouTube videos where you can see people harvesting roe from illegal white sturgeon. I don't know if these sturgeon murderers are ignorant of the exact regulations, but I do know they know they're supposed to have fishing licenses with sturgeon endorsements and that they're required to be aware of the laws. To make

FIG. 5. Bound smelt. Photo by Mark Spitzer.

an analogy, nobody goes out driving a car not knowing that a license is required, unless they're idiots, criminals, or just too young to know.

Fishing with Bartek and Lars I was eager to use my new twelve-foot Ugly Stik with a giant golden spincasting reel Penn had sent me for alligator gar. It was set up with hundred-pound braided test (PowerPro green), and Bartek showed me how to rig it up. Basically, it's a version of the Carolina rig: the line is threaded through a plastic cushioning bead, then poked through the eye of a swivel, another bead is added, and the line is tied to a larger swivel. Some lighter monofilament is then tied to the first swivel, and an eight-ounce weight is attached to that so that the weight can stay on the bottom and the fish can take out line. To the other swivel, we tied on a ready-made thirty-inch string leader

FIG. 6. Sturgeon rig. Photo by Mark Spitzer.

(130-pound test) and secured a 9/0 octopus-type hook. Circle hooks also work well, but whatever the case, you're supposed to use barbless when going for sturgeon.

Then came the trussing up of the bait. I took a fresh ten-inch smelt and ran the point through the back of its head and out of its mouth. I then made a loop with the leader, which I passed the smelt through tail first, until the loop was right behind its gills. I tightened the loop, or "half-hitch" as Bartek called it, then made a few more, working my way down toward the tail. At the end of the fish, I attached a pickled squid (aka "sturgeon candy") through that series of loops and pulled it all tight.

Chucking the rig as far as I could, I then brought in the line until it was tight. Bartek did the same thing with a similar rod and a reel, and Lars did the same on a lighter weight pole. After that, we brought out the lawn chairs and settled in.

People began to stop by. The first guy was the foreman from the

FIG. 7. The infamous Sturgeon Man van and curvy
public art. Photo by Mark Spitzer.

construction site, coming over to see how we were doing. He told us
he'd seen a lot of sturgeon caught off this dock in the last few days,
mostly by "the Sturgeon Man" who came by every day in his funky red
van. The foreman told us that the Sturgeon Man used a combination
of herring and live sand shrimp, which was good information.

An hour after that, the Flag Guy came over. He was a retired vet with
an NRA flag cap, and he was checking on the American flag someone
had set up in the corner where we were fishing. Apparently the Flag
Guy had set up a smaller flag a few months before on a piece of rebar
jutting from the dock, but after a while it disappeared. Then someone
set up a flag pole that was still there, but after a few months the flag
got tattered, so the Flag Guy brought a brand new flag for it. He was
having some trouble tying it, and none of the construction workers from
the site would come over and help him. They just sat there with their
cowboy boots on, he told us, doing nothing.

After that a woman came over with two little tots. The boy was scooting around on a bike with training wheels, and he came right over to us and started asking a million questions. He was three and a half years old and his sister was two. She was stomping around in a mud puddle and getting her socks wet because she refused to wear boots.

Then the Sturgeon Man showed up and parked his former fire engine, a reconditioned 1958 International panel truck, next to the whacko yellow sculpture, which a homeless guy was using as a windbreak to chug a twelve pack in a brown paper sack. He kept to himself, but the Sturgeon Man came over to talk to us, and he gave us a huge Tupperware container full of cookies and cakes and pastries. He told us he liked to donate baked goods to sturgeon fishermen.

After he left Bartek snagged a foot-long northern pikeminnow in the side. We were checking out its silvery length and pouty lips when the tip of my rod slowly began to bend. A few minor jouncy motions happened, which signaled a sturgeon. They suck the bait off the bottom in their tubular, protruding lips, then snuff around in the general area.

"Let out your line," Bartek advised.

I did, and the fish started taking off. It was a lot like gar fishing, but with sturgeon you don't need to wait as long.

"Okay," Bartek said, "it's your call now."

Having just gorged myself on binge-reading about sturgeon, I knew what to do, and it played out like a textbook example. I shut the bale, the tip began to bend again, and I hauled back—but not super hard. It was enough to prompt that barbless hook to slip into the fish's rubbery lips, and then I set the hook. WHAM! I felt the meat, I felt the mass, and I kept my rod high. It arced as I brought the fish in.

A few minutes later there it was, coming in upside-down, bright white belly gleaming in the sudden sun. That three-and-a-half-foot sturgeon was no match for my heavy-duty rod and line.

Leading the fish over to the bank, I handed my pole off to Bartek and ran down to the rubble below where the graffitied words "GANG FIGHT" were spray painted on the concrete abutment. I grabbed the sturgeon right behind the back of its head. It was mine! The hook came

FIG. 8. Spitzer with sturgeon, Bartek in background. Photo by Lars C. Larsen.

out easily, and I hoisted it up for the photos. We didn't bother to weigh this fish, but I figure it was eight to ten pounds.

Taking a closer look, I checked out the sharp bony scutes running down its back like stegosaurus spines. I also got a gander at its four funny barbels hanging down like an old man's whiskers in a cartoon. Its protruding vacuum-hose mouth was also a prominent feature, as was its shark tale, the diamond pattern on its side, and its overall cartilaginousness. Its color was luminous and pearly, more white than gray.

Then, saying goodbye to that bizarre throwback to the Jurassic, a species that hadn't changed much in 200 million years, I released it to spawn and grow ginormous.

"You're bleeding," Lars said.

I looked at my hand. It was covered in blood. Those razor-sharp armored plates had punctured my palms in at least three spots. But what's a little blood? It was a small price to pay for the thrill we all got, and I'd gladly do it again—especially for a bigger one!

It was eleven o'clock in the morning and I had already achieved my objective, so everything from here on out was a bonus. But since we still had a day and a half of fishing left, we got back to it.

Later in the afternoon, the rain having let up, Lars took off to get some coffee. Before he left, I joked that if we caught one on his rod while he was gone, I'd write that he missed his fish because he went off to get a fancy chai latté. Lars shook his head and laughed, but two minutes after he left, his rod began to gently nod.

Bartek grabbed it and let out some line. He waited a minute, then hauled back. It was on, and it was bending the hell out of that lighter rod, putting up a much bigger fight than mine. Bartek kept the line tight, brought the fish in, then handed the pole to me. He went down to grab the sturgeon, and as soon as he slipped the hook out, I reeled in and ran down to snap some JPEGs.

I got one while Bartek was holding the fish in the water by its tail. That sturgeon was nearly four feet long and probably close to twelve pounds. Then it thrashed and broke from his grip, but it didn't swim away. It was a bit dazed and trying to regain its composure. Either of us could have jumped in and wrassled it back, but we figured it was where it was supposed to be, its glowing white form working its way back into the Willamette.

"We've got some good news and some bad news," Bartek told Lars when he came back. "The good news is we caught another sturgeon."

Lars's face lit up.

"But the bad news," Bartek resumed, " is we caught it on your rod."

Watching our buddy's expression go from one extreme to the other,

Bartek and I couldn't help laughing. Lars's hurt-child look lasted only a second, and then we were all yucking together.

There's no freshwater fish on the continent more mythologized than the sturgeon, no doubt due to the fact that the bigger the fish, the bigger the stories it inspires. Various Native American tribes regarded this fish as embodying the spirit of strength and longevity. Those grandfather-looking whiskers combined with the fact that sturgeon often surpass a hundred years old add to this image, which is consistent with the way other cultures also view the sturgeon as wise. Hence the nickname "the philosopher fish." According to Howard T. Walden's *Familiar Freshwater Fishes of America*, "one thinks of the sturgeon as a kind of philosopher among fishes, as if its ancient lineage had bred, over the thousands of centuries, a curious old wisdom and a quiet acceptance of change."

The Nez Perce and other northwestern tribes have an involved history of fishing for white sturgeon, but there are more hieroglyphics in British Columbia. That's where cryptozoological creatures like Ogopogo originated in the oral tradition. Likewise, in southwestern Alaska, the aggressive, blunt-headed Iliamna Lake Monster (otherwise known as Illie) is reported to be ten to thirty feet long. The indigenous Tlingit people referred to this cryptid as the fish god Gonakadet and left a few pictographs. The Aleuts of the Aleutian Island chain on the most westerly reaches of the United States recall a similar fish-monster called Jig-ik-nak. It's suspected that white sturgeon inspired these tales.

As with Bigfoot or the Loch Ness Monster, reports of sightings exploded in the twentieth century. Witnesses alleged spotting monster sturgeon, mostly from planes, in 1942, 1963, 1967, 1977, 1987, and 1988.

The most mythic sturgeon in American consciousness, however, is embellished in tales of a goliath taking down a team of horses. Sometimes these horses (or oxen or mules, in other stories) are on shore, and sometimes they're swimming. Sometimes they're in the Snake River, sometimes the Columbia, but they always hail from the nineteenth or

FIG. 9. "Horse-seining, Columbia River, Oregon."
Anderson Scenic Post Cards, Portland, Oregon.

early twentieth century. Sometimes grandpa cut the ropes; other times it was too late.

These stories are most likely rural urban legends spawned by questionable photographs. One that appeared as a popular postcard might have inspired the horse-team story. The caption reads "Horse-seining, Columbia River, Oregon," and it's easy to see how someone could imagine the team literally horsing in a twenty-foot leviathan.

Then there's a popular picture of a giant sturgeon in front of what looks like a sixteen-foot skiff, taken circa 1930. This image is suspect due to the two-dimensional nature of both the sturgeon in the foreground and the guy in the background. Both are rather stiff, and there are some choppy darker lines around the fish's head and tail that don't make much sense. Also, where are the scutes on the sturgeon's back and the diamond-shaped plates on its side? Let's not forget that there once was a time in American pop culture when quite a few hoax postcards were in circulation: cowboys riding jackrabbits, trout larger than canoes, grasshoppers the size of cars— the heir to this tradition being the highly elusive jackalope.

Anyhow, this monster sturgeon was supposedly caught on the Snake

River near Ontario, Oregon, and it was reputed to weigh fifteen hundred pounds. No certain length has ever been attributed to this fish. According to the "Sturgeon Length/Weight Chart" (online at how-to-fish.com), a 1,506-pound sturgeon measures 167 inches, or almost fourteen feet. But as everyone knows, when a fish is in the foreground of a picture, it looks a lot larger than it really is. The experts often look to the size of the eyes to calculate the general age of a fish, since the eyes usually stop growing at a certain point—but the eyes of this fish are not visible. What's visible is the extremely large hump on its back, which is more characteristic of an adolescent sturgeon. I've looked at a lot of photos of full-grown sturgeon, and it looks as though they lose that hump after about five feet long and become more cigar shaped.

The thing about this image is that it's not completely unrealistic: white sturgeon *were* once this huge. Still, the *Audubon Society Field Guide to North American Fishes, Whales and Dolphins* lists the maximum length for the species at twelve feet six—which, unfortunately or not, is realistic for these times.

On the second day we decided to go for the big ones, so drove across the mountains for *Acipenser transmontanus*, which means "sturgeon across the mountains." The word *sturgeon* itself comes from the German verb *störer*, meaning "to root around" —which is precisely what they do as bottom feeders.

As we drove the roads became slushy with snow banks on the shoulders. Mossy rocks rose from the crust, busting up from the mantle, dramatic waterfalls tumbling hundreds of feet through the mist. The idea was to get out in nature for a less urban sturgeon experience.

It took a bit of effort to get to the parking spot, from which we hoofed along the railroad tracks. We then hiked to a deep, foaming eddy where Bartek had caught a six-and-a-half-footer a few years before from a boat. We, on the other hand, were shooting to fish from shore.

FIG. 10. Also, how come there's enough light to see the fish and inside the bow, but the man is a silhouette? "1,500 lb. Sturgeon, Snake River, Idaho," c. 1930. Photo by Wesley Andrews. Courtesy Tacoma Public Library, SIRLES-59.

Bartek figured we could cut through the brush, which was a jumble of blackberry brambles on a steep embankment covered with snow. We were each hauling a camp chair as well as a backpack and our rods, and it got pretty treacherous. Grunting and sweating and breathing hard, we finally stumbled and tore our way to the shore. We were in the wrong spot.

We could see the right spot a half-mile upstream, so Bartek took off scouting for a trail. We had to retrace our steps back up to the tracks, cursing the chairs and losing our weights, which got snagged on brush and lost in the snow. Eventually we made it to the top of a cliff where a soggy old lean-to was decaying into the earth. Bartek said it was a sturgeon shack. There was even a platform to cast out on. So that's what we did.

The place provided a gorgeous view of Beacon Rock jutting up from the other side like a primordial pterodactyl perch straight out of the Cretaceous. There were jagged peaks beyond, and the mighty Columbia was roiling beneath us at the rate of a hundred thousand cubic feet per second and kicking up whirlpools the size of school buses.

Consequently, every time we cast out, our lines got tangled together or caught on the scree. Nevertheless, we fished all morning using pickled herring and live sand shrimp, and we lost a lot of tackle and didn't get a single bite. But having already caught my sturgeon, I really didn't mind.

We moved on to another spot by the Corbett exit on I-84, a viewpoint with a parking lot where semis were idling and sightseers kept coming over and questioning us. I don't know why these people seemed more invasive than those we met in the heart of the city, but our nature experience was basically dashed.

"Maybe we should go back to our proven spot," said Lars.

Bartek and I agreed, which was pretty unusual for me. When I have a choice, I always opt to be out in the wild. But since the wild wasn't working for us, we packed our stuff and went back.

Three random sturgeon facts:

1. Feeding: In *Great White Sturgeon Angling* author Bud Connor writes that white sturgeon eat "ghost and mud shrimp, crawfish, sculpin, herring, smelt, shad, salmon, lampreys and clams." To this list, the University of California's fish website adds frogs, trout, and domestic cats. The *Montana Field Guide* website adds "worms, and considerable plant material" and notes that the white sturgeon "will eat almost any available organism." In *Familiar Freshwater Fishes of America,* Walden echoes this sentiment, recalling a white sturgeon that once swallowed "a half bushel of onions which presumably had come from a cannery or warehouse upstream."

2. Leaping: In the *New York Times* article "The Lofty Mystery of Why Sturgeon Leap," John Waldman states that sturgeon jumping "is one of the great mysteries of the fish world." One theory is that they're trying to splash off leeches or other parasites, and another is that recently swallowed crayfish are pinching their stomach linings.

Courtship is also considered, along with the idea of capturing air-borne prey and casting off eggs during a spawn. It's also posited that their splashing is a way to communicate with each other.

3. Aquaculture: In *Familiar Freshwater Fishes of America*, Walden claims that "artificial propagation of this fish is impracticable." This might have been true in 1964, but sturgeon are now being farmed with an impressive amount of success. The California Caviar Company, for example, boasts sustainable farming practices and no-kill policies. White sturgeon are raised in organic aquaculture environments (meaning no anti-antibiotics), and the roe is "extracted from the sturgeon using a harmless massaging technique then delicately rinsed using the Köhler Process." Their top-of-the-line royal-grade white sturgeon caviar can be ordered online for ninety-two dollars an ounce, plus thirty dollars for shipping.

When we returned to our dock, the Sturgeon Man was already there, kicking back and reading in his bright red, funny-looking truck. It was three o' clock in the afternoon, and we got our poles in as soon as we could. The bites came immediately, and within half an hour Lars hooked into one, and it put up one hell of a fight. The fish stayed close to the bottom, bending his lighter weight rod. It made a run upstream, and then it shot under the pier. We were afraid the line might rub against a piling and sever the connection, but Lars brought it back.

It wasn't the lunker we'd been hoping for, but it was a hefty four-footer and the largest one we'd caught together. Lars pulled it over to the rocks, and I ran down and grabbed it. Probably a fifteen- to twenty-pounder.

The best thing about this fish was that it completed the equation. Each of us had now caught a sturgeon, which meant way more than if I'd caught another one. In a sense, each of us had reigned victorious in the battle of Man vs. Fish, thanks to the easy access and generous bounty of inner-city sturgeon fishing.

Lars got his photo in front of "GANG FIGHT" and let his fish go. We all exchanged high fives, and buzzing hard, got back to work, sitting in our lawn chairs drinking local microbrews.

Bartek caught a little one, maybe fifteen or sixteen inches, just before the sun went down. We checked it out and threw it back, and then it was dinner time. A chicken was roasting in the oven. Dirty and beat, covered in burrs, we shot back to Lars's place, psyched to have met the sturgeons we released.

Of course, the story I wanted was the story of the ten-footer that didn't get away, but that's not what happened. Which is fine with me, because if you always get what you want, and if the river doesn't throw you a curveball once in a while, then you're not challenged to view things from a different perspective.

I was therefore forced to reframe the narrative I had envisioned. But to do this, I needed some guidance—or so I figured, or wanted to believe. So on my way to Boise, I decided to interview Herman the Sturgeon.

Herman lives in a giant tank in the sturgeon-viewing section of the Bonneville Dam's visiting center, which is in a concrete labyrinth of holding tanks for native fish from the Columbia River system. There's a hatchery there and some informational exhibits for kids and tourists and anyone who gives a damn about the dam. Or sturgeon.

It was early in the rainy morning when Herman came swimming over, completely indifferent to me but spectacular in sturgeosity. He was ten feet long, 450 pounds, and seventy years old. His girth was girthy, his spikes were spiky, and his gillworks were intricate with flowery folds.

"So what's the take-home message?" I asked Herman, for lack of a better question.

But Herman wouldn't even look at me. He just wiggled his whiskers and kept on going, taking all the time in the world.

And that's the message I gleaned from Herman: that whopper white sturgeon still exist—as evidenced by Herman himself—and that I'll get my chance for a bigger one in the future. Because we're all transitional

FIG. 11. Notice how Herman lacks the exaggerated hunchback commonly seen on younger sturgeons. Photo by Kim Chen, portlandlocalguide.com.

creatures now, living together as two worlds merge, the world of industry and politics and a wilder world of co-existing organisms—some of which tend to make oversimplistic generalizations. That's what Herman said to me by not speaking at all.

My point being: Despite the abuse leveled at sturgeon, the great white behemoths continue to exist, but only because we have made an effort to fix what we messed up. Otherwise they might only exist in Canada, or in extremely endangered subpopulations, or maybe not at all.

So we're lucky to have them—if not for balance, then at least for what they inspire in us. And the main thing they inspire in us is the knowledge that they're not myth—which is important at a time when 63 percent of the sturgeon species on the Red List of Threatened Species are considered "Critically Endangered." In fact, the International Union for Conservation of Nature claims that sturgeon are more critically endangered than any other species, and that four species are most likely extinct.

Meanwhile, the most monstrous North American species is right here in our own back yard. And it boggles my mind that there aren't hundreds of fisher-people lined up on those abandoned docks to pull them in and throw them back.

Sure, most of those fish are juveniles (just ask the Sturgeon Man), but they're still as large as any big pike or trophy salmon. With thousands of three- and four-footers swimming around under those bridges, the opportunity exists for taking advantage of a totally unique and highly active sport fishery, especially if you use medium tackle. And as I refound out on this trip, white sturgeon are not hard to hook, they're a blast to fight, and when you put one back in the water, you're releasing a fish that can reportedly grow to twenty feet long.

So hell yeah for urban sturgeon! May we always share this intersection, and may we always remain respectful of each other, then go our separate ways.

4

Snagging in the Ozarks

There's Nothing Not Weird about Paddlefish

As a kid, paddlefish terrorized me. I knew they were in the Mississippi River, where I envisioned six-foot-long, shark-finned monstrosities glaring up at me with beady, hungry little eyes. My father told me that they only eat plankton, but as a ten-year-old with baloney-colored skin, I figured there were always exceptions to the rule, and there were bloodthirsty man-eating exceptions down there that saw my limbs as free lunchmeat—so how could they resist? More than a couple of times, I found myself breaking into a panic and thrashing as I swam for shore.

I've seen this reaction in others as well. Paddlefish, gar, sturgeon—the larger the fish, the more they inspire fear. It's not what we know about these creatures, however, that makes our adrenaline suddenly surge; it's what we don't know. And in the case of paddlefish, their overall freakiness definitely adds to their grotesque effect. That crazy flat spatulated nose is so unlike anything we've ever seen on any other fish that our imaginations naturally picture this fish as some sort of alien life form. Not only that, but the primitive factor divides us even more, prompting the children in us to recoil from what we can't understand.

Of course, I'm no psychologist, nor a scientist of any kind. I'm a fisherman in awe of the narratives we tell ourselves about the strangest fish in our midst—especially the ones we're still trying to fathom. Like paddlefish, which have been on this continent for at least 300 million years. By this time, you'd think we'd know them better. But as with other prehistoric fish, we're taking our time dispelling the myths.

Polyodon spathula, or the American paddlefish, has been called a spadefish, a spoonbilled catfish, a boneless catfish, a duckbill cat, and a shovelnosed cat, due to its mostly scaleless, smooth-skinned hide. But it's not a catfish as common misinformation has it. As noted on Kentucky State University's website *Paddlefish & Sustainable Aquaculture*, "consumer willingness to pay more for catfish meat than other commercially caught fish" was a factor in creating this impression.

Nor is the American paddlefish a shark, nor is it a sturgeon. The paddlefish's body style lends itself to such associations, but the sturgeon is much closer genetically. Both paddlefish and sturgeon are part of the Acipenseriforme family, sharing a cartilage-based structure and a rubbery-appearing exterior. Other traits they share are that both are "broadcast spawners," have four nostrils, and grow pretty big and pretty old. Paddlefish are capable of reaching lengths of seven feet, weights of up to two hundred pounds, and ages over fifty years.

Both sturgeon and paddlefish are also prized for their roe. When the caviar trade laid waste to the American sturgeon populations at the end of the nineteenth century, the market began to experiment with paddlefish, which soon followed suit in terms of their threatened status. This made life tougher for spoonbills, and the paddle-range began to diminish. Twenty-six states used to have paddlefish, but now we're down to twenty-two, ranging from southwestern New York to central Montana and down through the Dakotas and into Texas. Meanwhile, they've been extirpated from Canada, and the U.S. Geological Survey lists them as either endangered or threatened in about half of their remaining range.

The American paddlefish has a cousin in Asia—but like the other four paddlefish species that are now extinct, the Chinese paddlefish may not exist anymore. *Psephurus gladius*, sometimes called "elephant fish" due to its conical-shaped proboscis, can grow to a whopping twenty-three feet! But none has been seen since 2007.

Here's where one paddlefish myth comes in. Until a few decades ago, people believed paddlefish used their noses to stir up sediment in order to facilitate chowing down on zooplankton and—as some sources have falsely reported—"sand fleas." Biologists have since deduced that the main function of the paddle-nose, or rostrum (which is a third the length of the fish), is to act as an electromagnetic antenna to detect the plankton they filter through their gill rakers. That long, flat spoonbill also has another function: to provide lift like an airplane wing, which keeps the fish's head up so it can plow through the water scooping up microorganisms. Also, it's not uncommon for a paddlefish to get its snout chopped off by a prop. Many have continued to survive without this highly useful tool.

Their flesh is excellent to eat, and a commercial market does exist where populations are strong enough. But even today it's not a very popular food fish. Back in 1902, David Starr Jordan and Barton Warren Evermann wrote in *American Food and Game Fishes*, "True, the negroes of the South have long held it in high esteem along with the channel cat and the goujon, but it is only within the last four or five years that it has had a market value."

In Arkansas, at least, that market value was three dollars per pound a few years ago when I bought some steaks from a local commercial fisherman. I rubbed them with olive oil and a mixture of paprika, cayenne pepper, and garlic salt and grilled them on the barbecue. The meat was firm and white with a porky texture like mahi mahi, and it didn't taste fishy at all. In fact, it tasted a lot like swordfish—another fish paddlefish are sometimes confused with for obvious reasons.

I picked Hippy up in the Missouri Ozarks. Last time I fished with him, we caught a bunch of gator gar fry in Texas and transported them up to Kansas City, where we released them in the Missouri River in an attempt to reintroduce them back into the region. Hippy, however, had changed somewhat. No longer was he that goofy, gangly, wild-bearded longhair with stinky feet and overalls. Being a goat-farming teacher in search of more work, he now had a respectable haircut and a relatively clean shirt.

This time we were bombing our way up to Warsaw, Missouri, "the Paddlefish Capital of the World." The Osage River had been dammed in that area to create Lake of the Ozarks and Truman Reservoir, home to the healthiest paddle-populations in the world.

Our professional guide was Steve Brown of Catfish Safari, who's been guiding anglers for big blues and spoonbills for years. Steve is considered one of the most knowledgeable and successful paddlefish guides this side of the Mississippi. He has gear, he has sponsors, and he's been on *River Monsters*, which was all we needed to know.

The first day we went out on Lake of the Ozarks. It was the end of March and the water temperature was in the mid-forties. Paddlefish start running upriver in the mid-fifties to lay their eggs, and reportedly, that's the best time to fish for them.

The winter had been brutal, dumping extra snow and ice on the state thanks to all the "polar vortexes" and "Arctic blasts" of late, so I was worried that we had arrived too early. But Steve showed us the images of paddlefish on the depth finder, and we could clearly see them clumping up. The "sows" were on the bottom, he said, and the guys were hovering above like a bunch of dudes at the bar, trying to get some action.

We found a good pod and Steve cut the power to his 225-horse Mercury and instructed us on how to snag them. Our super-thick Penn Slammer rods were equipped with Daiwa Accudepth Plus baitcasting reels rigged with hundred-pound braided test. We each had sixteen-ounce weights on the end, with a size-8 treble hook three feet up and another one a yard above that. The hooks were secured to our lines at the tops and bottoms of their shafts.

Steve then brought his brand new custom SeaArk catfishing boat up to trolling speed and told us to let out two hundred yards of line, which we measured with the line counters on our reels. The idea was that the weights would drag along the bottom, and then we'd pull those hooks through the pod, and when a line crossed over a paddlefish nose, its bill would guide a barb into its mouth. When that barb hit fish, the pull of the boat would set the hook.

We did that but failed to connect. So we tried again. And again. All morning and all afternoon we dragged those weights across the bottom. Hippy and I were learning the techniques. Like getting the other line out of the water as soon as a clicker started peeling out line. Like distinguishing snagging the bottom from snagging a fish. Like backing up and getting unsnagged whenever we got hung up—because we just weren't getting bites. Or nibbles. Which is an odd thing to call a strike, but that's the terminology.

I wasn't disappointed, though, because we still had another day left. And as all this went on, Steve provided information and told us plenty of stories about the state's official aquatic animal. One that I was particularly interested in was the story of the paddlefish bust.

It happened in 2013, a year before we arrived on the scene. Sixteen thousand snaggers were getting ready for paddlefish season in Missouri, which starts in mid-March and runs to the end of April. Close to eighty-five agents from the Missouri Department of Conservation (MDC) and forty special wildlife officials from the U.S. Fish & Wildlife Service were also in the Warsaw area, having been alerted by citizens. According to the article "MDC and Federal Agents Snag Major Paddlefish Poaching Operation" published on the MDC website, locals contacted the department through channels like the twenty-four-hour Operation Game Thief toll-free hotline, which was specifically designed to catch poachers.

According to Steve, the Russians were involved. He told us that there was a large Russian population working at the local Tyson chicken processing plant and that some of them were taking paddlefish roe out of the country in suitcases. MDC Protection Chief Larry Yamnitz was quoted in the article as saying: "The national and international popularity of

Missouri paddlefish eggs as a source of caviar has grown dramatically in recent years. . . . This is a result of European sources of caviar having declined from overfishing of the Caspian Sea's once plentiful and lucrative beluga sturgeon." Yamnitz added, "A common black-market price is about $13 an ounce. Therefore, a single large female paddlefish with about 20 pounds of eggs is carrying about $4,000 worth of potential caviar for black market sales."

Steve had leased a dock connected with the poachers, and he told us that local rednecks were being paid two hundred dollars apiece for pregnant females, then taking their eggs and throwing the rest of the fish away. But whatever the case, undercover agents, the Benton County Prosecuting Attorney's office, the Sheriff's Department, the U.S. Department of Justice, wildlife officers from eight other states, and the FBI rounded up one hundred suspects from Missouri, Colorado, Kansas, Illinois, New Jersey, Minnesota, Pennsylvania, South Dakota, and Oregon. The main violation for which these poachers were eventually indicted had to do with transporting paddle-eggs across state lines. The Missouri Wildlife Code strictly forbids this, and so does the federal Lacey Act.

Ultimately, what all this underscores is that the state of Missouri works hard to stock local waters as do other states trying to sustain their paddlefish populations, but then, because there's a demand for the roe, criminals come straight to the Midwest to recruit poachers to take out fish paid for by tax dollars.

It could be argued that due to a lack of true sturgeon roe—which is the purest cocaine of the caviar trade—paddlefish eggs are synonymous with a cheaper-grade street crack. For example, the caviar dealer Marky's sells an ounce of legal Missouri paddlefish caviar for twenty dollars an ounce, whereas Caspian beluga caviar sells for $280 more than that. At the time of this writing, their beluga caviar was out of stock.

In short, there are caviar dealers willing to pay millions to supply addicts whose habits know no environmental bounds. They don't care what effect their exploitation has on fisheries, because that's what they do for a living: killing for short-term gain. In the meantime, communities invested in the long term end up with anemic ecosystems that suffer from the loss of biodiversity. This happens all over the world in the contraband name of caviar, which is why sturgeon and paddlefish are struggling to survive from Iran to the American heartland. As the editors of *Sturgeons and Paddlefish of North America* assert in their overview of the situation, "The story of sturgeon and paddlefish extermination is one of human gluttony and greed. To be sure, it is one of the most telling ways in which humanity has failed in our stewardship of the planet."

But we've also failed in other ways.

That's what I couldn't help observing as we motored across Lake of the Ozarks, which has 1,150 miles of shoreline with seventy thousand homes on it. Traci Angel's book *The Scars of Project 459* documents the problems caused by this major construction project. The publisher's description of the book notes "poor water quality, loss of habitat, and increasing concerns about aging waste-management systems" as just a sample of the issues resulting from the building of Bagnell Dam.

And there we were, dragging the bottom beneath a horizon of multi-million-dollar mansions. There were yacht docks everywhere and marinas full of speedboats just waiting for the summer sun, at which time the snaggers would be replaced by thong bikinis, spray-on tans, and binge-drinking vacationers. This area is known for party-barge bacchanalia in which flotillas full of hot young bodies twerk unto the stars above—until someone drowns, which happens every year.

We've dammed this river to make use of it: to control flooding, to generate hydroelectricity, and to make places for jet skis, water sports, family fun, and all-day drug abuse. In pretty much every text I've read regarding paddlefish, the massive drops in their numbers are blamed on the unholy trinity of overfishing, pollution, and river modification—the latter being responsible for a culture that has severely impacted this fishery.

When the U.S. Army Corps of Engineers constructed these dams between 1929 and 1979, they knew that paddlefish would take a hit.

They'd get cut off from their spawning grounds, and since they don't climb fish ladders like salmon (because the metal rebar irritates their electrosensory receptors), it was basically a no-brainer that this already compromised species would suffer even more.

The solution was to stock the system extensively—and stock all the other systems as well. The Mississippi Interstate Cooperative Resource Association (MICRA) was therefore established in 1992 for the preservation of paddlefish and sturgeon. Committees were formed, goals were identified, actions were taken, and overall it has worked out pretty well.

As the Missouri Department of Conservation noted in a 2014 press release, "Artificial stocking sustains the reservoir fisheries. The quality of fishing varies from year to year because the Conservation Department stocks more paddlefish some years than it does in others." This press release goes on to say that in 2001, "the Conservation Department's Blind Pony Fish Hatchery produced its second-largest crop of paddlefish in history. More than 145,000 young paddlefish found their way into Missouri waters that year. . . . Then in 2008, a particularly favorable set of conditions produced the largest crop of all time, an astonishing 260,000 paddlefish."

But since none of those fish had graced us with their presence, Steve told us we probably wouldn't get any that day, even if we stuck it out. We'd gone eighteen miles upstream but couldn't find a pod with a big enough concentration to make it happen. It was the same thing with a guide Steve knew whom we kept passing. "If we're not catching them," Steve told us, "we're not catching them. And if that's the case, there's nothing we can do about it except try somewhere else."

It was too late in the day for that, however, so Hippy and I decided to concede.

The next day we got a late start on Truman Reservoir, but the look of this lake made me feel optimistic. The largest man-made lake in Missouri, it wasn't overdeveloped at all—just a few homes and a lot of bluffs and naked stumps sticking up. There were bald eagles soaring and diving and grabbing fish, and there were no other boats on the water. Just us, looking for the motherpod.

We hit the first fish within half an hour. The clicker accelerated, wound down, then surged forth again. I leapt up and grabbed that rod, clicked the clicker off, and hauled back while Hippy got his line out of the way.

It came in like a sack of rocks. I reeled in as I lowered the rod, then hauled back, repeating that rhythm over and over again. Two hundred yards later, we saw it come up, entangled in the line and snagged in two spots.

Steve slipped the gaff under its gill and pulled it toward the boat, where he grabbed its bill and hoisted it over the rail. Holy Crap! It was ours! I actually caught it! The pressure was off.

It was just over four feet long and close to thirty pounds. We didn't have a scale on board, but we did have a tape measure. It was exactly thirty-four inches from the eye to the fork of the tail, which is the minimum length for a keeper on these two lakes and Table Rock Lake and all their tributaries, whereas everywhere else in the state the minimum is two feet long. Steve said that since this fish was borderline, we should throw it back, just in case some game warden came around and contested it.

But first I took a good look. Paddlefish have some hard-to-see ganoid scales somewhere behind the head, but I couldn't find them anywhere. The nostrils, on the other hand, were clearly visible, shaped like small volcanoes behind each eye. I noted the flaring, sickle-looking gill speckled with delicate flowery patterns resembling cat-paw prints. There was also something human about its rotating eye, which was pretty much pleading with me, "Dude man, please put me back . . ."

I figured this fish was from the 2007 batch, which was now seven years old. According to that previously mentioned press release, "The 2007 year-class . . . should start providing a good number of legal, 34-inch fish weighing 25 to 30 pounds."

After I put that spoonie back, I noticed a peculiar white slime all over

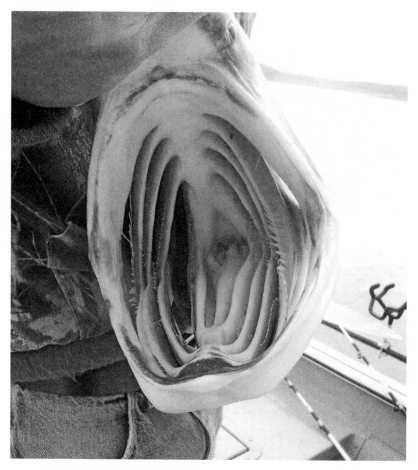

FIG. 12. Hippy's big paddle-mouth. Photo by Mark Spitzer.

my jacket. It wasn't the clear type one usually picks up from rubbing elbows with a fish. It was gummier and more opaque. It was paddle-sperm.

We motored around some more and eventually saw a colossal pod. They were bunched up at fifty feet, nearly a hundred schooling beneath us. That's when the next reel started screaming.

Hippy grabbed it while I shot video. He horsed it in, also bound up like the one I'd caught. It was pretty much the same size, so after we high-fived and took some pictures, Hippy let it go.

FIG. 13. Hippy and Spitzer with paddlefish. Photo
by Steve Brown of Catfish Safari.

Now we were buzzing and feeling good. The paddlefish were coming
in. Then I caught a small, iridescent blue cat. Just snagged it in the side.
Hippy caught one as well, not much larger than two pounds. It was a
good eating size, but snagging catfish is illegal, so we tossed them back,
hoping they'd survive.

An hour later, I hit my big fish. This one was snagged in the tail, so
it put up more of a fight, swimming away as I pulled it in. It was four
and a half feet long, about thirty-five pounds. We kept that one in the
extra-long live well.

After another couple cats that just happened to be in the wrong place
at the wrong time, Hippy hooked into the biggest fish of the day. It was
just short of five feet, and we figured it was a forty-pounder. That one
went into the live well too.

It was now late in the afternoon, and we couldn't find the jumbo pods
we'd seen earlier that day. We saw individuals scattered here and there,
but none of our trebles were connecting. We tried for a few hours, but
the only thing we saw was one lone goat on the water's edge, poking
around in the rubble. At first I thought it was a stray dog, but it was
definitely a lost goat. It looked at us, and we looked at it, and no words
were exchanged.

"Are you worried about that goat?" I eventually asked Hippy.

"Yeah," Hippy said, and we went on back with our fish.

Steve cleaned them on his dock with a Samurai-sized fillet knife, cutting off all the red meat and slicing out the mud-line. There was no roe, which meant they were males. We soaked the flesh in a bucket of cold water for half an hour, and in the end, we had thirty pounds of freshly caught paddle-meat.

But our trip wasn't over yet. We still had one more "field trip" to take. Osage Catfisheries Inc. was just an hour away in Osage Beach, and I'd made arrangements to visit their holding tanks. This aquaculture facility wasn't just the oldest American paddlefish farm in the world; it also boasted "green" caviar made "from sustainable farm raised Paddlefish." Their website stated that they were "the only C.I.T.E.S. (Convention on International Trade in Endangered Species of Wild Fauna and Flora) farm approved by the U.S. Fish & Wildlife Service," so we were definitely interested in what they had going on.

When we rounded the bend, we saw the ponds. The place was part fish farm, part golf course, which made sense considering what I'd read in a *Fortune Small Business* magazine article that was republished in *CNN Money*. It said that when these paddlefish reach an arm's length, they're moved into artificial lakes at real estate developments and golf courses across Missouri, where (we later learned) they're raised for more than ten years. When they're harvesting size (sixty to ninety pounds), Osage Catfisheries pays the owners fifty cents per pound for males and $1.25 per pound for females. The article explained that "Unlike farmed sturgeon, paddlefish require little care: They live off zooplankton that grows naturally in water. And paddlefish are fun to have around because they breach like whales, especially when a golf ball flies into the lake."

The office was surrounded by holding tanks. There we met another Steve—Steve Kahrs—dressed in waders. We sat down for an interview, and he told us this "paddlefish ranch" was part of a family fish farm that raises thirty-two different species, including Asian carp and alligator gar. The golf course was part of the equation, and the effluent from the tanks was used to water the grass.

I asked Steve if the paddlefish they kept in ponds were affected by fertilizers and insecticides, and he told me no, because all chemicals used must be EPA-approved. He also told me that no antibiotics are used, so the fish they produce are organic.

For more than three decades, Osage Catfisheries was the only paddlefish farm in the country, but now there's more competition driving the price down for spoonbill caviar. Osage Catfisheries used to ship millions of viable eggs to Asia in the early eighties but is now starting to move its caviar to clients in Russia. A small percentage is sold in the United States, and those profits go to charity for cancer research through an event called Heart's Delight.

I asked about research, since I knew that Osage Catfisheries was working with universities as well as aquariums. The *Fortune Small Business* article mentioned that the Kahrs family was "working with the Missouri Department of Agriculture and the University of Missouri at Columbia to extract paddlefish collagen for use in the cosmetics industry as well as medical applications such as cartilage and joint fluid replacement." Also, the University of Michigan's *Museum of Zoology Animal Diversity* website notes "a growing interest in the immune system of American paddlefish . . . [because] they rarely, if ever, get cancer due to their cartilaginous skeleton. . . . Therefore, American paddlefish have been a useful and promising test subject in the field of aquatic pharmacology." Steve replied that they were raising paddlefish for research, but he wasn't at liberty to discuss the specifics.

We circled back to the pond concept. I was curious about how much water a paddlefish needs. Steve told me that three to five fish per acre was standard. Most of the ponds they used were larger than five acres, which technically makes them lake-sized bodies of water with enough oxygen for the fish to survive.

As for the process, Osage Catfisheries was the first fish farm in history to spawn paddlefish successfully in a tank. Mostly, though, they use an *in vitro* fertilization technique in which paddlefish sperm and eggs are mixed for fifteen minutes using wild turkey feathers. The fertility rate is 90 percent, and the fertilized eggs go into hatching jars where they're kept for five to seven days at sixty degrees Fahrenheit. When the fry hatch, they're placed in nursery lakes for a year, where they're fed an artificial diet and planktonic blooms. After that they go into larger ponds or lakes, where they eat plankton and trout pellets until they're netted and harvested.

Steve then took us on a tour. We saw quarantine tanks where baby fish were being held, and larger tanks with sophisticated aeration systems. The caviar processing happened somewhere else and was closed to the public.

So that's what we learned that day: that paddlefish are being farmed in safe, productive environments that respect both fish and the ecosystem (since it's not impacted), and that the ongoing research is rich in possibilities.

In the car, heading down to Hippy's farm, I couldn't help reflecting on one nagging little detail that just kept bugging me. In a sense it was like that goat we saw staring at us from the shore. It was there, it existed, and it seemed to be provoking a question—so I decided to bring it up.

"Ya' know," I said, "every time we brought in a paddlefish, it sort of seemed anticlimactic . . ."

"Yeah," Hippy agreed, "paddlefish can't fight. They just come in like logs. That was weird."

"Exactly," I answered. "And it's a weird way to fish. I still don't know how I feel about snagging those catfish by accident, and I keep wondering if this sport is really a sport. I mean, we didn't burn one calorie trolling out there for two days straight."

"But we got 'em," Hippy said. Then he added with a laugh, "Paddlefish are weird."

It was such a simple, spot-on statement that I couldn't help laughing too. Still, I wanted to know why he thought they were weird, so I asked him to elaborate.

"Because they're these gentle, ancient vegetarians swimming around looking like blimps," Hippy chuckled. Then holding his hand flat in front of his nose, he said, "And they've got those weird schnozzes, and those weird pieholes gaping wide open as they tool around, sucking stuff up. And they've got weird nostrils and weird gills. There's just nothing *not weird* about paddlefish."

Again we both laughed. Again, it was true. As true as the fact that American paddlefish are now in the Danube, having escaped from fish farms in Romania and/or Bulgaria. So now they're running wild in Serbia, Russia, Moldavia, and who knows where else. And they're getting by. But they're also being farmed in the Czech Republic, Hungary, Ukraine, and a bunch of other Eastern European countries.

Why? Because paddlefish have staying power, with the potential to go totally global. Because paddlefish can adapt, and we want what they've got—especially if they can cure cancer. Because paddlefish are undeniably, indisputably, and irrefutably as weird as a fish can get.

5

Alien Invaders in the West

This Isn't Kansas Anymore

When it comes to "Asian carp" (a class that includes common carp, grass carp, black carp, and silver and bighead carp), the North gets all the attention—thanks to bighead and silver carp threatening to destroy a $7-billion-a-year industry in the Great Lakes. The questions up there are mainly: Are they here yet? Can they reproduce? And how can we stop them? We've been asking these questions for decades in the South and Midwest, where Asian carp populations have been increasing exponentially since the eighties, meaning the destruction isn't something that might happen in the future—it's happening right now, and it's moving west. What's at stake, of course, isn't just the Great Lakes region—it's our entire continental ecosystem.

As usual, we're distracted by the continuous struggle of economies versus the environment. We focus on the Chicago Area Waterway System, which is the link between the infested Mississippi and Lake Michigan. There's a multimillion-dollar electrical barrier in there that sends out pulses these fish don't like, but they're still sneaking in. According to the Asian Carp Regional Coordinating Committee (a coalition of federal and state agencies), the Obama Administration has invested $200 million in trying to stop this plankton-algae-eating plague, which is actually causing bigmouth buffalo, gizzard shad, and paddlefish to become skinnier and less healthy due to competition for resources. Plankton-eating mussels and shrimp that other fish feed on are also becoming more anemic, which has its effect on the food chain. So in 2009, fearing for their fisheries, the state of Michigan filed a lawsuit against Illinois to shut down the Chicago Sanitary and Ship Canal in order to keep Asian carp out of Lake Michigan. Minnesota, Indiana, New York, Ohio, Pennsylvania, and Wisconsin got involved as well as Canada. Then in 2010 the United States Supreme Court decided in favor of jobs over the environment and ruled that the canal would remain open for business.

Meanwhile, the most prolific of these introduced species, the notorious silver carp, has been running amok from Florida to North Dakota and down to Texas, with occurrences in Nevada and New Mexico. Dubbed "the flying fish" because they can shoot ten feet out of the water at the sound of motorboats, they've been smacking boaters and water-skiers upside the head and creating a general nuisance. A kayaker was knocked out of a race in western Missouri in 2010, a jet skier broke her back in 2003, and an inner-tubing teenager in Arkansas got his jaw busted in 2008. These stories are as numerous as online videos showing these fish (mostly in the range of five to fifteen pounds) erupting like popcorn and causing calamity.

Recreational activities aside, businesses are bummed out too. For example, the dredging outfit Kaw Valley Companies, Inc. was recently "in a protracted, increasingly violent conflict" with silver carp on the Kansas River. I saw this story in an issue of *Kansas City Business Journal* and called the company's vice president in an effort to confirm that "they jump right out of the river and slap workers on his boat." I couldn't get a reply. Ultimately, the company claimed it had to spend "$10,000 on a new boat with a cab that can protect" crew members.

The broader safety concerns, however, are more environmental in scope. Invasive carp have been weakening our systems by moving in and forcing other fish out. Silver carp reportedly eat between 20 and 80 percent of their body weight per day, and they're reproducing at alarming rates. Being able to reach weights of a hundred pounds, bighead and silver carp are currently laying waste to ecosystems by redefining the landscape of our waters and what they contain.

So I shot off to Kansas to see this problem for myself.

I had arranged with Jessica Howell—the Aquatic Nuisance Species program coordinator for the Kansas Department of Wildlife, Parks and Tourism (KDWPT)—to sample silver carp at the confluence of the Missouri and Kansas rivers in Kansas City, Kansas. We met at the Kaw Point access at 10:00 a.m. Chris Steffen, the Commercial Bait Program coordinator for KDWPT, and Jessica Edmunds, their seasonal commercial bait technician, were also on hand.

Admittedly, I was excited to get out in the field with them. Still, I had to tone it down a bit, to avoid appearing anxious to capitalize on their state's misfortune. After all, this wasn't a fishing trip—this was serious research regarding an urgent eco-concern.

We hopped into their flat-bottom boat and tried the Missouri River first, but nothing was happening. It was late April, and Chris figured that the colder, deeper waters in the Missouri were concentrating the silvers in the warmer waters of the Kansas, so we tried there, revving as we followed the shore. We were aiming to stay in about five feet of water, where Jessica H figured the carp were.

The person in the stern, they told me, gets hit most by flying fish. That person was Chris, who joked that since this was Jessica E's initiation into the Aquatic Nuisance Species program, she'd be taking a hit for the team. But then came another joke, which was basically leveled at me—something along the lines of "Thanks a lot, Arkansas, for providing us with yet another invasive species to deal with."

It was true. Though originally from China and Russia, bighead and silver carp had escaped from fish farms in Arkansas back in the seventies. United States invasions of black carp (which can reach lengths of seven feet) and grass carp can also be attributed to Arkie negligence. My response to the question of "Who let the carp out?" was to acknowledge that Arkansas had also bumbled the snakehead, the most notorious invasive aquatic species this continent has ever seen.

We soon hit a school and the silver carp started leaping all around us. Most of them leapt back toward the stern, always shooting willy-nilly, but some were leaping in front of us. There seemed to be no logic to their direction or velocity. Some vaulted straight up, others at random angles. Some leapt eight feet, some leapt two, and some leapt in a series of rapid bursts, torpedoing in and out of the water. Some shot away from the boat, some rammed it head on. We were constantly hearing gonging thuds under the hull as Jessica H, in the bow, tried to nab them with a net.

Every time they leapt, it was a blast. None of us could keep from cheering when a big one broke the surface. Sometimes they'd rocket right past our heads, barely missing us. Other times, we'd feel the prop connect with one underwater.

Then one landed in the boat and started flopping. It was a three-pounder, all pearly and pretty and shining whitely. What made it grotesque was its bony, scaleless head, eyes positioned down by the jaws. We put it in a bucket.

As we followed the shoreline and circled the pylons supporting the bridges leading in and out of downtown, we talked about how scientists can't explain why silver carp act so jumpy in American waters. In China, they don't leap as much, even though this characteristic is part of their identity. Centuries ago Asian carp were known for leaping over waterfalls known as "dragon gates," which inspired a proverb about students facing examinations. The idea is that if a student can pass a test like a carp leaping a dragon gate, then that student can ascend to the next socioeconomic level.

Jessica H had been working with silver carp for years, mostly in South Dakota. She theorized that the smaller ones jumped more than the larger ones because they're more gregarious. When they get older and larger, they don't school as much. Jessica also suspected that they released a pheromone when they leapt, triggering a communal reaction.

She then gave up trying to net them in the air and took over driving

FIG. 14. Jessica Howell of KDWPT and Spitzer
with silver carp. Photo by Chris Steffen.

the boat, throttling down then throttling up, working those fish into a
frenzy. She handled that boat with expertise, and I was glad to try the
net, and so began a series of misses that soon surpassed forty-something,
always missing by just a few inches.

I'd seen videos of what's commonly referred to as "redneck fishing," in which yahoos wearing football helmets tear through schools
of leaping carp, either netting them or smacking them with baseball
bats. Sometimes these people are on water skis, but mostly they're in
boats. There's even an advanced form of this practice in which archers
shoot silvers in flight.

Since it's pretty much impossible to catch a silver carp on rod and reel
(because how do you hook phytoplankton?), it was clear that netting an
airborne silver was the closest to sport fishing that I was going to get with
this fish. But I just kept missing, which greatly disgruntled me. I figured
that if things continued in this vein, then all I'd be was along for the

FIG. 15. Filter-maw made for "ram-feeding" on
microorganisms. Photo by Mark Spitzer.

ride, not playing an active part. Also, I couldn't really count a fish that
leapt into the KDWPT boat as a fish I caught myself, which is always a
goal when I investigate a fish. The bottom line: I wanted one, dammit!

So when a huge one leapt within range, and I saw it ripping toward
me and kicking up spray like a mad dolphin pumped up on steroids, my
senses sharpened and instinct took over. It leapt, I lunged, and due to
my sheer desire to get that fish-missile, I made a split-second calcula-
tion and thrust the net into the spot it was heading for. The carp went
straight in, T-boning the boat with a massive THWAAK! When I lifted
the net, there it was.

We'd only been out on the water for an hour, but it was the largest
silver carp we would see all day: thirty inches long and ten pounds. What
a rush! My mission had suddenly been accomplished.

We caught a couple of two-pounders after that, just tooling around.
They leapt into the boat as Jessica E and I shot videos of carpfield ballis-
tics. Then we went back to the launch, where Chris caught another carp
as we circled below the parking lot, waiting for the truck to back down.

FIG. 16. Ready for battle. Photo by Chris Steffen.

The law requires that these fish be killed immediately, so after we pulled the boat out, I dispatched them with a knife. The biologists then collected data on the fish we had caught, recording their weights and measurements. Since I had a Kansas fishing license and my catch was legal, I asked Jessica H if I could take the one I caught back to Arkansas. She said sure, and threw in the others as well.

Chris and the Jessicas then departed, leaving me to clean my fish, cutting off as much red meat as I could find. And let me tell you, those hard-boned fish are hell on fillet knives.

I was now prepared to do battle on my own, armed with a trashcan lid and a motorcycle helmet. My vision was to go blasting through the jumping jihad, deflecting fish left and right until I filled my salvaged, bat-finned 1959 Whitehouse Runabout to the rim. I had even built a frame around my fish finder to protect it from atomic slaps of fishular mass.

The first place I went was downstream on the Missouri River to where an outlet from a sewage treatment plant was churning up thousands of tons of water. I wondered if the silver carp would be there, but they weren't, so I went back to the Kansas River. I plowed around for a while in the same spots I'd been to previously, but for some reason the fish just weren't leaping as much.

A few theories came to mind. First, perhaps there was something about the outboard engine on the KDWPT boat that was different than mine. Theirs was a sixty-horse Mercury, whereas mine was a twenty-five-horse Yamaha, but that shouldn't make much of a difference. Whether using a two-stroke or a four-stroke, videos on YouTube show motors of all sizes scaring up silver carp.

Second, maybe my fiberglass hull had something to do with the lack of leaping fish. The KDWPT boat had a metal hull, which might vibrate differently and spook the fish more. Or third, maybe it was the shape of my V-hull. Possibly flat-bottomed boats send out different reverberations than hulls that cut through the water more.

Whatever the case, the silvers weren't venturing close enough to my boat to land in it. However, some did jump, which allowed me to ogle them in flight. With fewer fish leaping, it was easier to focus on one at a time, and I was always astounded by their strange beauty.

I also saw other species: loads of nesting geese, two owls flapping around on the bank, and a bunch of dead fish, including a reeking thirty-pound common carp. Those carp were our original invasive carp. German carp got loose in the United States in the 1800s, and they're virtually everywhere now, playing a role in countless ecosystems, where they destroy gamefish nests and suck up eggs—which is why there's a firmly established culture in America of leaving them on the shore for the flies. It's a controversial statement, but I'd say we've struck a kind of balance with this particular invasive species, which is pretty much under control. That is, we've learned to live with it throughout its range, and it doesn't really cause that much trouble—at least not compared to other members of the Cyprinid family.

Still, the reputation of the common carp has affected those of the silver and bighead. Since the common carp is not prized for its meat, the general public perspective is that our newer Asian carp are also not good to eat. The word *carp* is associated with the lowliest of our "garbage fish" and is not a stellar selling point.

After an hour or so of driving in circles on the river, wasting gas and polluting the air, I began to feel a bit self-conscious. To anyone watching from the shore, I must have appeared like someone with too much time on his hands who didn't have anything else to do except annoy those looking to nature to provide a sense of calm in their lives.

So I gave up and went back, tail between my legs. It was an anticlimactic ending to a day of dealing with a planet in decline as I strapped the *Lümpabout* to its trailer and hit the interstate east. But as Kansas and its carpy conundrum began to fade in my rearview mirror, that feeling became more of a frustration.

Even though I got my fish, I never got a fix on what this pox meant for Kansas, which like other states is dealing with a host of other invasives—zebra mussels, silver perch, noxious weeds, Dutch elm disease, Eurasian milfoil, etc. If anything, I was left with more questions than I came with—including what makes the struggle with invasive species in Kansas different from that in, say, Florida?

The only answer springing to mind was recognition of the fact that we're fighting more invasive species these days than ever before. We have different species with different dynamics in different places, but one thing we all have in common is that as this battle for resources compounds itself, we're being forced to employ more financial resources to help preserve our natural ones.

This wasn't a consoling thought. It was vague, and it lacked the substance I was looking for. I wasn't making sense of anything. I was just noting what everyone knows.

But then I saw a sign.

The sign said "City Market," so I got off on the Missouri side and found myself in the other downtown Kansas City. If I could find a fish market, I figured I might gain some more insight. After all, that's what "freshwater detective" Jeremy Wade does when he's looking for clues.

It was a Tuesday afternoon, and I couldn't find a single fishmonger. I did, however, stumble into a place called Chinatown Market. I was hoping they'd at least have some canned Asian carp, but the closest I came was a whole frozen snakehead—a fish I'd always wanted to try.

Something just made me buy that packaged snakehead. It was from Vietnam, it cost $5.84, and I threw it in the cooler with the silver carp.

Then, driving south on 71, I couldn't help considering the popular attitude toward this truly grotesque invasive species as compared to how we regard Asian carp. Whereas the U.S. government decided to let Asian carp roam free rather than shut down shipping in Lake Michigan, our reaction to the snakehead has been the exact opposite. When snakeheads were discovered in a Maryland pond following Y2K, 9/11, and the anthrax attacks, the paranoid public freaked out. The snakehead was depicted as an all-devouring, land-roving, un-American monsterfish, and we began a campaign of poisoning any body of water where it might be. We had highly elaborate fishkills for snakeheads in North Carolina in 2002, in downtown Chicago in 2004, in Queens, New York, in 2005, in Pennsylvania in 2008, in Virginia, Wisconsin— kill, kill, kill!

In fact, we had the hugest orchestrated "fish purge" in history in Arkansas after a federal ban on snakeheads was enacted in 2002. Dunn's Fish Farm near Monroe had drained a pond to kill their snakeheads, and they didn't figure that since snakeheads can breathe air they could squiggle into drainage ditches, which was what happened. By 2008 they were breeding in Piney Creek, and they were at the forefront of the U.S. invasive species crusade. Over a hundred wildlife officials from multiple states suddenly showed up in "the natural state" with helicopters, ATVs, and a fleet of snakehead slaughter-boats. More than 49,000 watershed acres and 440 miles of tributaries were treated with rotenone, resulting in a hundred snakeheads being killed and fifty more being caught.

I went snakehead sampling the following summer. The biologists I accompanied failed to find any in the streams we depleted of oxygen, but they were still being found in the vicinity. Killing everything in the system had definitely weakened the snakehead populations, but the sad fact is that they're still out there reproducing. This is never announced on the evening news.

So why this disparity? Why are we terrorized by snakeheads to the point of action, but not driven to go after invasive carp with the same passion? The answer, I think, mainly has to do with scale. Asian carp have taken over half the country, so we feel defeated, which leads to non-action. Also, and more important, we just don't feel that threatened by silver and bighead carp. To us, they're just big dummies, and non-aggressive ones at that. Snakeheads, on the other hand, are way more grotesque. We view them as vicious child-eating *frankenfish*, a word that became popular in 2004 when the Lou Diamond Phillips movie of the same name came out about giant, mutant snakeheads going postal in Louisiana.

Snakeheads, however, may not be as furiously destructive as Hollywood and the media make them out to be. By the same token, invasive carp may not be as benign as we believe them to be when we think of them as happy, hopping novelties. Or, as a counter-argument, silver carp may not be as destructive as we fear them to be as they work their way across the country. Though "Asian carp now make up 90 percent of the fish biomass" in some places in the Midwest, Ray Petering of the Ohio Division of Wildlife notes, "Asian carp have not wiped out other species in the Mississippi and Illinois rivers." This observation comes from a 2010 article in the *Columbus Dispatch* in which Dr. Konrad Dabrowski notes that Asian carp were introduced in Poland "without harmful consequences . . . to control algae and other unwanted life forms." Dabrowski adds, "There are populations of Asian carp in Europe that are 40 years old and never spawned." Meanwhile, some scientists argue that invasive carp cannot reproduce in the Great Lakes, while others argue that they can.

What we need to do is get the facts straight and get a consensus, which is hard with a fish we know little about—even if bighead and silver carp are the most farmed fish in the world. The Chinese have been raising them for over a millennium, and they're in Europe, South America, India, Pakistan, Puerto Rico, and at least sixty other countries.

What our Asian carp confusion echoes is the climate change "debate," which has confused the public to the extent that some people believe there's a debate when there's not—which, of course, is the intention of the confusers. Debating climate change, of course, works for those at the top of the dragon gate by suggesting that the unified voice of the scientific community is merely leftwing propaganda. This tricks those who can't make the leap over the dragon's gate into thinking that short-term, trickle-down gain is more important than long-term sustainability. By constantly dismissing the findings of science and claiming that there are authorities on the right who've debunked the idea of human--induced global warming (when there's no credible research whatsoever that supports such claims), the confusers manipulate the populace into not knowing what to believe. When conscienceless corporations fight for advantage in the marketplace, we get politics rather than facts—to the extent that politics are mistaken for reality. It's not about what's right for the environment; it's about how certain parties are *justified* in their actions—which has nothing to do with *justice* at all.

Similarly, there's a lot we don't know about invasive carp, and this ignorance can cripple us—which is why it's good that there are programs and experts and movements out there trying to educate the general public. But we need to know more, and we need to know it faster. Like how can we incorporate dead zones to keep invasive carp out of the Great Lakes? Or is there a way to attract them or repel them en masse based on pheromones or sonic vibrations? Acoustic vibrations that utilize "velocity fields" that carp can't breach are currently being employed in Iowa and studied at the University of Minnesota, so that's another possibility.

Research is key. And so is vigilance. And so is outreach. And creative solutions, like eating them, because they're delicious.

It's an idea that many have tried, starting with the Chinese, who've been using silver carp as a major source of food and traditional medicine for over a thousand years. Reportedly, the meat has a codlike taste and is scallopy in texture.

In the United States, the if-you-can't-beat-them-eat-them approach has been slowly catching on. A commercial industry has been developed in Illinois, where Asian carp made up 82 percent of the state's commercial fishery in 2008. Most of the millions of pounds produced annually are shipped to Asia. Some is processed into gefilte fish for sale in Israel and the United States.

A few states have flirted with the idea of feeding Asian carp to prisoners, but this has been slow to catch on. What is catching on are humanitarian efforts like the program Target Hunger Now! Working with the Illinois Department of Natural Resources, Chef Philippe Parola of Baton Rouge has been conducting silver carp cooking demonstrations. He prefers this fish over tilapia for its clean, non-muddy taste and the fact that since silver carp don't eat other fish, they're low on mercury. Hence, fishermen are donating Asian carp to Target Hunger Now! and the program feeds thousands of needy children and families each year.

Still, the stigma of the word *carp* hinders public acceptance. That's why some rebranding has been in the works. Silver carp is occasionally referred to as "Kentucky tuna" or "silverfin." In Minnesota there's been an effort to call them "invasive carp," but for reasons that have nothing to do with the commerce of food. This particular rebranding is meant to avoid provoking bias against Asian people through negative associations with an invasive Asian fish—a campaign reminiscent of squawfish being renamed "pikeminnow."

But there are also technical concerns affecting the popularity of Asian carp, which, if transcended, could provide the opportunity to feed the American mainstream cheaply, rather than just the poor. After all, there once was a time in American history when lobster was believed to be fit only for prisoners.

Jackson Landers's 2013 article "How to Stop an Invasion of the Easiest Fish in the World to Catch" from *Slate's Animal Blog* proposes a partial solution to marketing Asian carp. "The trouble is that there is still no network of local processing plants near the Missouri River capable of processing silver carp into the types of food products that the American market will buy," he writes. "Carp have unusual bone structure compared with most other fish, and they require different technology to process." Thus, Landers asks, "What if, instead of spending hundreds of millions of dollars on barriers that will eventually be circumvented, we spend 10 percent of that money on a few processing plants? With a market that would pay 25 cents or more per pound, commercial fishermen would be able to make a reasonable living ridding the water of silver carp."

Landers is asking the right question, and there's definitely something to what he's proposing. But to be sure, it was obvious what I had to do next.

For Invasive Species Night, I thawed out the snakehead and removed it from its package. The fifteen-inch fish was totally intact, all eely-finned and razor-fanged with murderous bulging eyes. I filleted two nice slaps off both sides (leaving the ribs on, as I did with the carp) and was amazed at how easily the meat came off. I then cut out the mud-line running horizontally down the middle of both pieces and removed the red meat. Like the silverfin the night before, I soaked those fillets in cold water for a half hour to remove any impurities.

I then mixed up two marinades. For the silverfin I started with two bottles of teriyaki sauce (no high fructose corn syrup), then added soy sauce, garlic salt, some Vietnamese garlic chili sauce, and a shot of water to thin the mixture. For the snakehead I mixed a bottle of gluten-free Thai peanut sauce with a green curry paste, soy sauce, minced garlic, and some white wine. After covering both fish with their respective sauces, I placed them uncovered in the fridge to marinate all day.

As for the snakehead's snaky head and spine, I placed that on a plate and put it on the beer shelf of my refrigerator to greet my guinea pigs—I mean guests—when they arrived. I even propped its fangy mouth open with a toothpick to show off its needly teeth.

FIG. 17. Snakehead after being filleted. Photo by Mark Spitzer.

My test subjects arrived at six o'clock, and something was wrong with the propane grill. For some reason the flames were wimpy, and I couldn't get the temperature to rise above 300 degrees, so I had to cook medium-low and medium-slow, which worked out pretty well. I put the snakehead on the top rack, cooked it for ten minutes with the cover closed, then put the silverfin on the bottom rack and cooked those pieces for about seven minutes on each side while constantly basting. When the carp meat started falling apart, I knew the fish was done.

Basically, the sauces were so intense that it didn't matter what the fish tasted like. People preferred the denser texture of the snakehead over the silverfin, which was flaky like crappie, not like scallops at all.

But the bones also played a part, especially in the silver. Not really knowing how to clean the fish properly, and not having enough meat to be that picky, and being comfortable eating bony fish, I'd imposed my vision on my guests. A few of those nine food-testers didn't like dealing with the bones, but for most of them, it was worth the effort.

At the end of the meal, I asked everyone if they'd buy these fish to cook themselves if they were commercially available. Everyone said they'd definitely buy the snakehead, but a few weren't so sure about the carp. "What if you could buy the silverfin deboned?" I asked, and that changed the entire equation. Everyone said they'd buy the carp meat if it was deboned.

So there you have it: a sample population from among 300 million Americans was pleased to eat two very different invasive species. Not only that, but all indications suggest a demand ready to be fulfilled for the supply that's out there right now.

I've caught flak before for my position on invasive species, mostly because I believe in rolling with the punches rather than fighting losing battles. In this high-traffic world of transporting exotic and non-indigenous species for profit and practical application (like controlling algae or insects), invasive species have become unavoidable. There's no guarantee that we're entitled to live an invasive-free existence, especially when hypo-critical humans are the widest-ranging invasive species on the planet. I also believe that we can strike a balance with nonindigenous species and incorporate them into our cultures and grow as a people by making lemonade. And after considering the invasive carp/snakehead situation, I'm even more entrenched in this position.

We can freak out, erect faulty fences, dump hundreds of millions of dollars into programs that may or may not slow our descent into hell, or we can do what makes sense. So let's be real: what makes the most sense with Asian carp is to consume the problem before it consumes us. Because there they are: millions and millions of tasty, versatile, readily available, high-protein, mercury-free fish that can feed millions of people. It would be plain foolish *not* to take advantage of this opportunity—especially when we have the means to control the expansion of this invasive while conserving our native ones at the same time.

So in seizing the day, let's seize the carp—and provide a new context for *carpe diem*!

6

Nebraska, Bowfin, and
the $8,000 Bullhead

Or How to Catch a State Record Fish

When I officially proposed this book, I wrote, "My goal with this chapter is to employ my Arkansas bowfinning skills (I catch them all the time) and my history of knowing this fish to land the Nebraska state record—which I believe to be in Dead Timber Lake, where the current state record was caught over thirty years ago." Admittedly, this was a ridiculous claim to make, seeing I knew nothing about that lake except that Ronald Evenson had caught an eight-pound state record there in 1982. Also, I knew that bowfin were scarce in this region of the Great Plains. Being indigenous to North America, they're native to some places in Canada, but in the United States they range from the Atlantic coast to the Dakotas, and from there you can pretty much draw a vertical line from Grand Forks down through the eastern edge of Kansas and into Texas. Hence I was cutting through Missouri, en route to Nebraska.

The bowfin is a boneheaded prehistoric fish that's been around for about 100 million years. It doesn't get much longer than three feet or more than twenty pounds, but pound for pound, it's the fiercest fish I've ever fought. Bowfin thrash like insane tarpon, sometimes leaping six feet in the air, and when you get them in the boat, they smack all around. Pinning down a bowfin is like trying to restrain a juvenile delinquent and can sometimes result in a black eye or bloody nose.

As opportunistic carnivores, bowfin share the same diet and habitat as gar. They like slow-moving backwaters just as much as lakes and river bends, plus swampy terrain and buggy bayous. Bowfin have lunglike organs that allow them to breathe air, so if creeks go dry, they can burrow into the mud and wait for the rains. They're armed with razor-sharp canines, and they have long, eely dorsal fins running two-thirds of the length of their missile-shaped bodies.

Their coloration varies. Sometimes they're camo-colored, sometimes they're silvery, sometimes they're olivine or brown. When the males spawn, they're an electric avocado-lime-green. And wherever these uniquely grotesque "living fossils" swim, fishermen hate them because they're a nuisance to get off the hook, and they offer little value as food.

But not me. I've been catching these fish for over forty years. The first one I caught, when I was a kid in Minnesota, was a foot long, and I got it in Minnehaha Creek with an onion-sack net made with a clothes hanger and a broomstick. I chased it down in just a few inches of water, zigging and zagging all over the place, and I managed to nab it. We kept that fish in a tank for years, its dorsal fin rippling as it hovered in place.

After that, I'd catch them accidentally while casting for bass or bobber-fishing for sunfish, because that's the way they're commonly caught. I had an epic battle with one in my twenties beneath a spillway in Minneapolis in which I fought that bowfin more in the air than in the water. My buddy Kris Hansen eventually grappled it and battled it to the death, so to honor it I had it stuffed. It's on my wall as I type.

In fact, there are two bowfins on my wall. The other is a hefty ten-pounder I found in a flea market on the outskirts of Springfield, Missouri. The sign said "Bowfish," a word I'd never seen before. They wanted sixty bucks, so I broke out my credit card.

Now, in Arkansas, I catch them every week it seems—sometimes on trotlines, sometimes on jugs, sometimes on yo-yos (spring-loaded limb-lines) or rod and reel. I've caught them up to fourteen pounds.

So that's what I was after, heading up I-29. And that's when my engine blew.

I bought the "Existential Midlife Crisis Mobile" six months earlier, during a painful divorce. Basically, I needed something to focus on that didn't make sense, because that's what made sense to me. It was a 1980 Dodge Brougham motor home, nineteen feet long with an extended fiberglass body, a bathroom, a kitchen, a couch that turned into a bed, and a gaudy coppery retro-upholstered interior. I flew to Atlanta to get it, took a shuttle bus to Athens, and the guy picked me up. Without even driving the rig I paid $3,500 on the spot then balled that 360 v8, four-barrel Mopar monstrosity home. It only had forty-six thousand miles on it, so I figured it would make the journey.

I was wrong, and so were all my friends who encouraged me to go for it. I broke down in Memphis, and from that moment on, just about every time I took it out I had to get towed to a shop that charged me hundreds more dollars. Another $3,500 later (new carb, tires, stereo, alternator, starter, fuel pump, AC, etc.), I was taking it on my first actual fishing trip with a salvaged pirogue (small flat-bottomed canoe) strapped up top.

But when I pulled off to get a Whopper, something smelled funny. I saw that the radiator was overheating, so after I nursed it to an auto parts store and bought some coolant and a couple of jars of Stop Leak, I poured the stuff in and got back on the road. It stopped leaking, but then the engine started clacking, so I pulled off at a truck stop in Faucet, Missouri, knowing my engine was toast.

The tow truck guy took me to a place in St. Joseph called Dip Stix. I met the manager in the morning and gave him my sob story, and they got it into the shop. A few hours later the diagnosis was not as bad as I had feared it would be: the flywheel was cracked, and I needed a new radiator. They said they could get the parts that day and get me back on the road.

But that was not how it went down. The flywheel came in, but the radiator didn't, so I had to spend the night at a motel. Then in the morning they told me the radiator that had come in was wrong, and a specialized radiator had to be made by a welding shop in Kansas City. This point became moot, though, when they discovered metal shavings in my oil. The engine was shot, and putting in a new used one would cost $5,000.

I had to make the call. Would the $7,000 Existential Crisis Mobile become a $12,000 investment just waiting for the tranny or differential to go, or would I abandon this ten-mile-per-gallon gas guzzler before I gambled my life savings away? I chose the latter course and scrapped it for a hundred bucks.

There was nowhere to strap the pirogue to the rental car, so I had to abandon that boat as well. Still, determined to make it to Dead Timber Lake, I transferred all my gear and took off.

Was I bummed? Of course. Having spent $400 more on a rental Impala and $400 for the mechanic's labor on top of the $7,000 I'd already put into a van that turned out to be a piece of crap, I felt as if I'd just given $8,000 to a complete stranger.

So now there was even more pressure to get a bowfin, because if I didn't, then I'd be a double loser. That's what I thought, bombing up Highway 275.

I made it to Dead Timber Lake at around 5:30 p.m., and there was no one in the campground at all. I grabbed a spot right on the water, got myself a cold beer, and took a look.

It was an ox-bow lake so jam-clogged with waterweeds that if anything could live in these "hypoxic conditions," I knew bowfins could. It was shallow and mucky and full of what looked like fish highways cutting through the dense vegetation. Every once in a while one of these would open into a ten-foot circle filled with splashing catfish and playful turtles.

I cast out a pole baited with packaged shad, *splat* right into the lake, and then another with a liver on a treble hook. A beaver came by, I saw a garter snake, and there were rabbits and squirrels racing all over. I threw in a fish trap and a minnow trap to see if I could catch some bait.

Within half an hour I had a fat bullhead full of roe in the fish trap, which I used for bait on one of my heavy-duty gar poles. Then I caught a brilliant red-bellied painted turtle and cooked a can of beans and a Polish sausage on the campfire.

When the dusk turned dark, I dropped a battery-powered bobber right off the bank where there was a break in the weeds. I caught another bullhead and put it my bait bucket. Then I caught another one. They were all pregnant females, gobbling hard. I figured I'd catch a mess of them, use some as bait, and eat the others.

Later that night I hooked something bigger. It put up a fight as I pulled it toward shore, where it twisted hard and got off. All I saw was a white belly bent like a horseshoe in flight. It was about a foot and a half long. I took another glug of whiskey, crawled into my sleeping bag, and reclined in the front seat as far as I could.

In the morning the catfish were going berserk. They weighed five to fifteen pounds each, and they'd surface, roll, thrash, then motor straight down with their tails sticking up, usually in clumps of two or three, rubbing against each other. Farther down the lake I saw something huge leap straight out of the water. It was about three feet long and had a long yellowish belly; it could have been a bowfin.

I walked down that way and cast a headless bullhead into one of those catfish clearings. When it hit the water, five or six big cats flinched in its vicinity. I left my rod there and kept on walking, then came to another clearing in the weeds. If the winter hadn't gone on three weeks longer than usual that year, this hole would've been even more overgrown with weeds and definitely inaccessible by now. But since it wasn't, I could see some sunnies swimming around. I also saw some bass, and then two shortnose gar, so I tried fishing that spot for a bit. Nothing happened, and I kept on going. On the other side of the road was a small pond. I saw a school of carp cruise by and eventually caught a crappie for bait.

Heading back to the campsite, I noticed that the big cats didn't give a dang about the bullhead I had deposited in their midst. They were distracted by spawning, I concluded. Walking the bank in the other

direction, I peered into the open spots, taking note of the various species. I saw skinks on the shore and minnows in the lake but no bowfin
whatsoever.

Later in the afternoon I went to the other end of the lake and set
up two poles. I walked that area and saw all sorts of fish but again no
bowfin swimming with their snouts sticking out of the water, forming
a wake—which is why they're sometimes referred to as "beaverfish."
But, of course, a watched bowfin never boils.

I found myself back at camp, sitting in my lawn chair, bemoaning the
whole situation. Basically, I was out eight thousand bucks, I couldn't
be sure if there was a single bowfin left in this lake, I was dirty, I was
tired, and I didn't feel like spending another night sleeping in the car,
only to end up bowfinless.

I considered checking out the Elkhorn River, where a train had wiped
out in the 1800s, spilling a bunch of non-native American eels into the
system. The marshy environment of Dead Timber Lake, however, was
probably more conducive to bowfin.

To kill time, I got up to clean my last bullhead to add to the others
I'd cleaned the night before. I figured I'd fry them up for dinner. But
when I opened up that bait bucket and took a look at that puny sucker
wiggling its whiskers at me, I just couldn't bring myself to do it.

Little did I know, this was the best decision I could have made.

There's no way I can write about bowfin without going into a linguistic
spiel, since they're known by a host of names—especially by anglers
who think they're reeling in a bass, only to discover a bowfin on the
other end. Up north, they're called dogfish, no doubt due to their lowly
status and solo wolfy nature, devouring whatever they come upon and
making off with bait. Down south, and especially in Louisiana, they're
called cypress trout because they're commonly found in cypress swamps.
But they're also called *choupique* there, a Choctaw word that literally

means "filth-fish"; the fish books prefer the translation "mudfish," also commonly used.

Bowfin have been called swamp muskie, brindlefish, blackfish, shoe-pike, cypress bass, scaley cat, buglemouth, German bass, spottail, grinner, cottonfish, cabbage pike, mudpike, speckled cat, lawyer, and ling. They are called lawyer and ling due to being confused with burbot, which bowfin resemble. Of course, bowfin are also sometimes confused with snakeheads, but that's an entirely different fish family. The bowfin (*Amia calva*) is the only remaining living member of the Amiidae family.

My favorite word for bowfin is what we call them in Arkansas: grinnel, with its derivatives of grindle, John A. Grindle, and brindle. I suspect this name evolved from Grendle, the monstrous beast from *Beowulf*. The Bowfin Anglers' Group website states that "The spelling 'grindal' was used as far back as 1709, when English botanist John Lawson encountered the 'soft sorry fish' during his explorations of North and South Carolina." This site also notes that grindle and its different spellings come from a German word for "ground" or "bottom" as well as an obsolete English word for "a narrow ditch or drain." "Grindle-tail, a breed of dog in 1600s England," is a possibility too. But the connection I like best, also considered on this site, is the word *grindel*, "an Old Norse word meaning fierce or angry," which circles back to my *Beowulf* theory.

Speaking of theories, here's another. Biologists have found more females, older females, and bigger females in population studies of this fish. For the most part, they think the reason is that the males expend more energy making nests and guarding the young, which somehow makes them more vulnerable. But there's something else that might make the difference: the *ocellus*, or eyespot on the tail. It's black and surrounded by a burst of orange. All bowfin are born with this spot, but only the males retain it. Biologists figure that it's a defense mechanism and that when predators see this spot, they think it's the eye of a larger fish, and hence they refrain from attacking it. But what if, let's say, the defense mechanism works in a totally different way and provokes territorial predators to attack? It could be posited that this eyespot distracts predators from the female bowfins and lessens the pressure on that gender so that they can continue to produce about twenty thousand eggs per shot to be fertilized by surviving males.

I can already hear the moans from my colleagues in the natural sciences, whom I challenge to disprove this theory. If they can do so, we'll know way more than we do now, and the truth is we don't know much. As with gar, research on bowfin has been limited due to the fact that "management efforts have focused on eliminating this fish." That's what Jonathan G. Davis's 2006 thesis on bowfin at Nicholls State University states, along with the fact that "the ecological role of this species is not fully understood." Davis notes that understanding these fish better would be beneficial for studying "the structure and function of floodplain ecosystems" and maintaining balanced fish populations.

There are other species that depend on bowfin as a vital ecosystem niche. As Davis's thesis states, "Bowfin, along with gars and shad *Dorosoma* spp., accounted for about 57 percent by volume of food for American alligators *Alligator mississippiensis* in Florida." And then there's the global bourgeoisie, who, faced with a dearth of sturgeon and paddlefish roe, have been open to a market for "Cajun caviar," which I've made myself through a guerilla brining process. The homemade stuff is actually quite edible (for the first couple of days), which explains why a commercial market for a higher quality product supposedly exists for bowfin in the lower Mississippi regions.

What I can't understand is why there's a commercial market for bowfin meat. It's not a big market, but it does exist, and bowfin meat, quite frankly, is the worst fish I've ever tasted. I've tried cooking it in all sorts of ways, and there's just something about it that's not right. It has a spoiled-tasting barky bite that always leaves the toxic tinge of fetid intestines in your mouth. Gray and maroon, the meat also gets mushy fast. Soaking it in milk never helps, nor does cutting out the mud-line. Personally, I've given up cooking this fish, even though there are loads of traditional recipes posted online.

My friend Keith "Catfish" Sutton, the biggest B.S.er I've ever met, once told me a story about a fishing camp somewhere down south. Every day the fishermen would go out and catch fish and bring them in, and

Ol' Cookie, the chef, why he'd cook those fish right up. But one day
Ol' Cookie went out fishing, and he caught himself a big ol' grinnel. It
was ten pounds and three feet long! So Ol' Cookie decided to cook that
grinnel up, and he put it on the grill, and he covered it in onions and
peppers and garlic and all sorts of stuff, and that's when the fishermen
started coming around. At first they laughed at Ol' Cookie and made
fun of him for cooking a grinnel. But then they got to smelling what
Ol' Cookie was cooking up, and then they started salivating. Everyone
wanted to try Ol' Cookie's grinnel. So Ol' Cookie told those fellas,
"Y'all can have a taste, but not till I'm done eating my share." So they
watched Ol' Cookie cook, and finally he took his fish off the grill. Then
everyone gathered around, mouths watering, and Ol' Cookie sat down
and started eating. And he ate the whole thing.

"What?" I asked after a pause. "That's the end of the story? That's
what you've been making me wait for?"

"Yep," Catfish laughed with a big grin on his face. "He ate that whole
ten-pound fish and no one got nothing except Ol' Cookie."

So I was sitting there getting sunburned and skunked, knowing I was
not going to catch a bowfin that night, because if there were any bowfin in this lake I would have seen one by then. I was cursing myself for
making the grandiose claim that I could catch a state record fish, when
suddenly the story took a radical turn.

Yep! I thought of that bullhead in my minnow bucket, and I pictured
its yellowish underbelly. *It could be a yellow bullhead*, I thought. But as I've
found from studying the three subspecies, the color of the skin doesn't
always reveal what kind of bullhead you have. What really matters are
the barbels.

I'd found this out from missing four state records in Arkansas.

The first one happened with a spotted gar. I caught it on Lake Conway on a chicken liver, and it was definitely a seven-pounder. But since
some tourist literature I'd read from the Arkansas wine country said

the state record was eleven pounds, I threw it back. Then I went home and looked it up and found out that the eleven-pounder was indeed the state record . . . but for bow and arrow. On rod and reel, it was only six-pounds-something.

The second time, I caught a calico-looking brown bullhead on a yo-yo, also on Lake Conway. Because this wasn't an uncommon catch I threw it back. Later I looked the fish up and saw that it was a brown bullhead, and the species wasn't even listed in the Arkansas record book. So I figured I'd keep the next one I caught. Years went by and I never caught another one. Then someone else did and got the record.

The third fish I missed was a pirate perch, which is a little purply bass-type fish, which I caught in my minnow trap. Since this fish didn't have a listing in the state records, I called up Game and Fish, but they told me a minnow trap doesn't qualify as "unrestricted tackle," and that pirate perch, being just a few inches long, weren't even worth considering. My friend Catfish, however, had formerly worked for Game and Fish as the official state record keeper, and he told me he had written those rules and that pirate perch were legitimate. Whatever. I gave up on that fish.

Then one day I caught a yellow bullhead. Since this fish wasn't listed on the Arkansas Game and Fish Commission state record website, I took it into the local office, where a biologist measured and weighed it. We looked up the details and it definitely met the description. But to be sure, he went and checked the database. And guess what? There actually was a state record from back in 1957 or something. Why wasn't this information available to the general public? Hell if I know!

So operating on a hunch, I checked out my last bullhead, which was the smallest of the six or seven I'd caught on Dead Timber Lake, maybe half the size of the largest I'd caught. It definitely had a yellow sheen, especially under the jaw and down toward the tail. Since I had a printout of the Nebraska state record fish with me, I then looked it up. They had a listing for black bullhead, and a generic listing for a plain old bullhead (back when all bullheads were considered to be of the same species), but no yellow bullhead.

Hmm. I had to know more. I called my trusty sidekick Scotty, who happened to be sitting in front of a computer. I asked him to Google "yellow bullhead" and "identification." He told me that yellow bullheads had white barbels under the chin and a rounded tailfin.

"Thanks," I told Scotty, and went back for another look. She had the rounded caudal fin, but the under-barbels were pale and pink, not white. So I figured it was a black bullhead, because that's the color it mostly was.

But sitting there not relishing the thought of another lonely night not catching bowfin, I recalled the black bullheads of my youth, and how they always seemed to be just black and white. Not yellow anywhere.

Okay, I couldn't just fritter this opportunity away. I packed up my stuff, hooked the minnow bucket up to a bubbler, and drove to the town of Fremont to find the public library. I got on the Internet and started double checking. After a few Googles I landed on the *Michigan Fishing* webpage for yellow bullheads at fishweb.com. The fish shown had the exact same coloration as mine and the rounded tail. It said the barbels are either white or pale or pinkish. I then checked the other bullheads on the site and saw that the brown's tail ended in a vertical line and the black had a slightly forky quality, less spatulated than the yellow's tail.

The determining factor came down to the rays in the anal fin. I went to another site and found out that yellow bullheads have twenty-three to twenty-seven rays. Then, out in the parking lot, I counted the rays on my bullhead: twenty-five!

I immediately went back inside, looked up the phone number for the Nebraska Game and Parks Commission and called them up. After a few transfers I was connected to a guy named Daryl in Fisheries. He said the fish would have to be verified by two state biologists, but since it was Friday afternoon, they'd be closing in an hour, so I could come back on Monday.

I considered this for a few seconds. Whereas I could spend the entire weekend on Dead Timber catching even bigger bullheads, I really wanted to get home. Daryl provided directions to the office in Lincoln. A few minutes later, I was back on the road.

That rental Impala got up to 110 in only a few seconds. When I saw

FIG. 18. Spitzer with monstrous state record yellow bullhead. Photo
by Daryl Bauer, Nebraska Game and Parks Commission.

the speedometer registering this, it scared me enough to slow down to
seventy. I got lost once, which took ten minutes off my time, but I made
the forty-nine-mile drive in fifty minutes and arrived in the parking lot
ten minutes before they closed.

"Yep," Daryl said when we put it on the scale, "that's a yellow bullhead."

Two more biologists came in and confirmed what he said.

Daryl then gave me a form to fill out and told me that I'd be receiving
an official state record certificate in the mail.

Holy crap! One grotesque had led to another. It wasn't the state record
bowfin, but it was definitely an official state record fish, something I'd
always wanted. Sure, it was only nine inches long and six ounces, and
after it was listed, someone would no doubt come along and say, "Hey,
I catch those all the time," then go out and beat my record. But for the
time being, I was the state record holder!

But was a state record bullhead enough to justify not catching a bowfin? I had to keep asking myself, driving east toward Omaha. The answer, though, was obvious: *Who the hell cares!?*

I was buzzing hard from having accomplished one of my objectives in life. I was calling up family and friends as if I'd won the lottery—and, in a sense, I had. Once again, in searching for the story, the story had found me. And once again, it was a story I never could have generated from my own imagination even if I tried. In this story Chance had called the shots—to the extent that losing my ludicrous motor home was damn well worth the price I paid. That's what I kept telling myself, even if there was really no logical connection between blowing an engine and catching a hornéd pout. Because that's what happened in this story, a real-life narrative in which our hero transcends the blows delivered to him and ends up in the top rung of Nirvana.

Catching a state record, I learned, isn't always about catching a bigger fish than somebody else; sometimes it's about identifying a species correctly. When I told Daryl I was surprised nobody had brought one in before, he replied that most people don't know how to identify yellow bullheads. It was the same case in Arkansas, where we also have an old generic bullhead on record, and the brown and yellow bullheads weren't even on the books until just a few years ago.

The assertion that most people don't know how to identify a yellow bullhead was reconfirmed when I stopped at a moldering Econolodge for the night just south of Kansas City. I got on their wifi system and did some more Googling. The first hit for "yellow bullhead" was *Wikipedia*, which claimed they could grow up to forty-five pounds.

No way! I kept Googling and found out why. Some guy had caught a forty-five-pound flathead catfish that was yellow in color (in fact, they're sometimes called yellow cats in Texas), and he'd gone on some Internet chat room claiming he'd caught a world record yellow bullhead. The extensive conversation that followed was basically a debate as to whether that fish was a bullhead or a flatty. And there was also another debate that had gone viral on Facebook. Someone had caught a yellowish channel cat (its identity evident from the forked tail) and had also claimed his fish was a record-breaking yellow bullhead. This had caused a lot of chatter that, when combined with the alleged forty-five-pounder, had provoked more Internet hits for "yellow bullhead" than a credible site ever could. Thus people were trusting social media over science when identifying yellow bullheads.

That's why I went to the International Game Fish Association website and got the right information. The world record is actually 6.6 pounds. I then took that figure, went back to the *Wikipedia* page, and edited the entry with the correct information. Still, by the time this paragraph sees print, I bet that someone convinced of seventy-pound bullheads swimming among us will refalsify that information.

I had won! I had definitely won—there was nothing else I had to prove. Nevertheless, we're all conditioned to want more. So after trucking Grendel8000 back to Arkansas and setting her up in a ten-gallon tank, I called for an emergency meeting of the Fishing Support Group. This term is a joke, but the purpose behind it is quite serious: it's an excuse for my buddies and me to go fishing.

We met at Bates bait shop in Mayflower for a bowfinning expedition: skinny, grinning Scotty with his eternally unlit cigarette tucked behind his ear; long and lanky Turkey Buzzard, a boldy bald chemistry professor; and my old pal Minnow Bucket, master of "the Mexican worm-line." We brought two canoes, loaded up on minnows, and shot down to Grassy Lake, which is a slough beneath Lake Conway, notorious for copious bowfin.

The water was way up thanks to recent rains, so we could really get around in there. It's easy to get lost in that labyrinth of jungly tupelos and cypresses bordering the flooded fields, but Minnow Bucket had a handheld GPS device.

We took off, paddling through the moccasins, herons, turtles and beaver dams, throwing out jugs and noodles as we went. All of them had lines and weights and hooks attached. Our bait was goldfish, trotline minnows, bass minnows, and chicken livers.

After we left a trail two miles long, we found a levee, got out, and did some fishing. At one point we smelled a dead fish and followed it to its source. It was a bowfin, shot with a bow and arrow.

"Hey, Bully," T. Buzzard yelled, applying a new nickname on me because I caught that record bullhead, "here's your bowfin. Want to take a picture with it?"

"Nope," I answered, "we gotta catch one ourselves."

FSG is a communal activity, especially with jugs and noodles. One person baits as another person paddles, and maybe someone else pulls the fish up while another nets it and another unhooks it. So if FSG catches a bowfin, it's technically *ours*. But for something like this, I could claim it as my own. They knew I needed a bowfin in order to resolve this chapter, and they were willing to help a brother out.

Anyhow, it became time to paddle back, and the first noodle we pulled up had a bright beautiful bowfin on it. Its belly was electric yellow, it had a blazing eyespot on its tail, and its pectoral fins were tinged with that neon spawning-green. Having thrashed itself into exhaustion while we weren't around, the fish had most of the fight knocked out of it. In fact, it was half-drowned and in need of CPR when we found it. This made it easy for me to manhandle the hook out of its throat. I crunched a few gills in the process and might've gripped it a bit harder than I needed to, but as I've learned, if you don't hold a bowfin tightly, it can crack you in the face. It was two feet long and about five pounds.

"Mission accomplished!" I openly gloated, and we kept on paddling.

None of the other lines had anything on them, and by the time we got back to the launch, our bowfin was deceased.

Turkey Buzzard, however, had been wanting to mount one for a while, so he put it in a cooler and took it to the taxidermist. And a few months later he had it on his wall, embodying a radically different version of the tale I just told. But that's another story, one having to do with a renegade red spot on its tail in addition to the eyespot, which he had the

FIG. 19. Spitzer with F S G bowfin. Photo by Scotty Lewis.

taxidermist recreate according to a photograph. F S G ended up giving Turkey Buzzard a lot of guff about that, and as far as we're concerned, the matter is still unresolved. But I'll let Turkey Buzzard tell that tale himself. The upshot of *this* story is that there's always an exception to the rule, and sometimes . . . a watched bowfin *does* boil.

7

Fear and Noodling in Oklahoma

How I Came in First at the Okie Noodling
Tournament Then Saw the Belly of the Beast

Somewhere along the line I went from the idea of facing my fears head on to hiring a legendary noodling guide, actually entering the world's most famous hand-fishing competition, and bringing in a professional photographer to shoot the whole experience. By the time my old traveling pal and cameraman Rob Butler and I arrived in Oklahoma, I was pumped and buzzing hard, ready to thrust my arm down any hole, no matter what lurked inside.

We met Skipper Bivins, star of the Animal Planet series *Hillbilly Handfishin'*, at Mac's gas station and convenience store in the small town of Walters, along with his wife JoAnn and full-grown son Christian. Their family business is known as Big Fish Adventures, LLC, and they're the first hit you get when you Google "noodling" and "Oklahoma."

I chose their outfit primarily for two reasons. First, I'd always liked the wise fatherly character I'd seen on that reality show. Skipper is a burly, jolly, colorful guy who likes to joke around with the city slickers he guides to the gates of hell. And second, I liked the idea of fishing mostly with my feet rather than my arms (in case I need to scramble for air), which is the technique Skipper's family had perfected through the generations.

Rob and I signed our waivers, and then we were off to grabble for flathead cats—which are truly the most grotesque catfish in the American West, or anywhere on this continent. With those beady little eyes and those large, flat, extraterrestrial-looking heads equipped with heavy-duty lower jaws, these top predators have been reported to reach weights of over 150 pounds.

When we got to the lake it was overcast, so I figured I didn't need a t-shirt or hat. Like Skipper, I wore blue jeans and two pairs of socks. No gloves or shoes to get tangled on underwater snags.

Skipper slid into the vast, mucky, stump-filled lake followed by Christian. They're both huge dudes, six two and six three, over 230 pounds each, and Skipper is as hairy as a grizzly bear.

I followed, and JoAnn and Rob brought up the rear. In the inflatable raft Rob was pulling, we had his cameras and lenses, some life jackets, a first aid kit, and a cooler full of Gatorades we'd never open, even though we'd be out in the ninety-plus-degree heat all afternoon; the lake kept us cool.

Skipper was moving swiftly, looking for holes he's known all his life, hogging for behemoths in these streams and lakes. It didn't take long for him to find a den and show it to me. By feeling the opening, he could tell it was uninhabited, which was fine with me, especially when he told me to stick both legs in and take a breath. The next thing I knew, Skipper was shoving me down into the hole, and I was feeling around with my feet. The tunnel opened into a cave in the clay, so I got a feel for how the nests were constructed.

I was able to stay down there quite a while, having practiced holding my breath for the last few months, sitting on my couch. I could always go for at least a minute, and once I even held it for two. Still, I figured that when I got into a catfish hole and there was physical stuff to do while holding my breath, the terms would be different. But they weren't. I found I could stay down there for pretty much a minute straight feeling around and using my arms to pull my body deeper in.

Knowing that Skipper was there to yank me out was definitely a calming factor, but I was also in the best shape I'd been in for more than twenty years. I had lost twenty pounds and decided to go for fifteen more through eating less and being a vegetarian for lunch. Just two days before I'd also met my lifelong goal of a hundred nonstop push-ups, which involved a lot of breath-holding concentration. So basically, I was physically as well as mentally prepared to "catfist" a big old flatty.

Let's get some of those other noodling verbs that I haven't yet mentioned out of the way. There's graveling, grappling, dogging, deepthroating, and cooning. Stumping is also sometimes used, and so are cat-daddling and hand-grabbing. But whatever you call it, it's the science and art of locating an active catfish nest, using yourself as bait, then horsing a catfish out. There's a controversy about whether this is ethical, but lately, more and more states are legalizing noodling because it's a culture that thousands have petitioned to legitimize at a time of ever-increasing popularity.

Noodling hit the mainstream in the early nineties and exploded on our consciousness when the documentary *Okie Noodling* came out in 2001. For the first time in history the urban myth of guys pulling catfish out of bayous with their bare hands was suddenly before millions of viewers, who saw for themselves that noodling was real. Then came *Hillbilly Handfishin'* and the National Geographic Channel series *Mudcats*. One of the stars of the latter is Skipper's younger brother Scooter, whom Skipper taught to hand-fish. Skipper claims Scooter is the second best noodler on the planet.

The world's top noodler then led us out to the main part of the lake where we found ourselves swimming if we weren't pushing through neck-deep water with two-feet of pudding-thick sludge on the bottom. We were constantly crashing into submerged logs and jutting rocks, but after a while I learned how to forge ahead cautiously in a ballet-type of way, bouncing off the bottom.

We went about a mile and I picked up the technique quickly. We were searching for clay banks, and when we found them we'd follow them and feel around with our toes for tunnels. The openings were either right on the top of a bank or on the side, and whenever we found one, Skipper would dive down and check the situation out. If there were dry bits of crumbly matter, that meant the nest hadn't been used in a while or someone had been feeling around in it, so its inhabitants were probably gone. But if the opening was clean and slick, that meant there was a cat in there fanning its tail.

"This one's slick as a cat's ass," Skipper said. "Might be a seventy-pounder in here. Come on over here, Mark."

I went over and descended into the hole, which was on the side of a clay bank about five feet beneath the surface. This took some fancy maneuvering, because after going down vertically, I had to go in horizontally, feeling with my feet. Totally submerged, I stopped at my waist. The water was colder in that deep dark hole, and my nerves were telling me to get out. Still, I figured I could weasel in further, so that's what I did, pulling myself in up to my chest—but I couldn't find a fish at all.

I came up and we trudged on for another mile—to a spot Skipper had marked with a stick.

"Oh yeah," Skipper said, "there's one in here."

He was sitting down, his head just above the water, and he pulled me right in front of him and sat me on his lap. With his feet blocking the outside of the hole, my feet were poised at the threshold. It was reassuring to have Skipper right there, and it was also reassuring to know I could breathe air and skootch on down. Then suddenly, WHOMPF! the fish attacked, chomping down hard on my right foot.

I flinched but refrained from pulling out. I did exactly what Christian told me to do, which was work my other foot into the fish's mouth and pry its jaws open. I felt them flex to their max, and I knew I had that soccer-ball-sized maw in a fully locked-open position.

I told Skipper I had the fish, and he told me to back out until the fish was in the opening. When I got to that spot, he dove down, ran the stringer through the mouth and out through its gills, then came up and wrapped the other end around my hand. This is the part you never see on TV.

FIG. 20. First blue cat. Spitzer on left, Skipper on right. Photo by RJB Photo.

Rob got in position with the camera, and then Skipper said, "Alright, pull it out and hold on."

The fish came blasting out of the hole and shot straight to the surface, where it erupted all over the place, slapping water ten feet through the air. I held on as it freaked out, then pulled it over and hefted it up. It was a blunt-headed blue, a male that had been guarding the nest, because that's what they do. From the skin grown over one eye, we figured it had been hooked before. It was pushing twenty pounds.

Hand-fishing for blues had recently been legalized in Oklahoma, and the Okie Noodling Tournament now allowed any species of any fish to be entered, but it was too early in the game to settle for this one. Though the Chamber of Commerce website said that any fish caught after noon on this day was legal to enter, the Okie Noodling website said that a fish had to be caught after six o'clock to be a contender. Whatever the case, I decided to let it go, figuring we'd find more. Skipper put the fish back in its den.

We went about three or four miles across the lake, checking holes and talking about all sorts of stuff. The word on the noodling street was that the prior year's Okie Noodling champ was not legitimate. The

FIG. 2 1. Lucy Millsap. Photo by Sarah C. Phipps. Courtesy of the *Oklahoman*.

seventy-two-pounder was alleged to have been caught on a trotline, because it had a freshly punctured lip.

Lucy Millsap had caused quite a stir when she brought in that enormous flathead. She was a nineteen-year-old cheerleader from Texas, and the fact that she competed against the men rather than entering the women's category chapped a lot of macho hides; her competition reportedly cussed at her.

Skipper told me that some people catch cats on trotlines and hold them in tanks until contest time. He also told me that sometimes whopper catfish get used for multiple tournaments. Lucy Millsap's cat, he said, was all scuffed up from being held in a cage and was used in several different competitions. He said it was not uncommon for people to buy and sell trophy catfish for the express purpose of winning noodling competitions, which are now popping up all over the place.

Bradley Beesley, the brainchild behind the film *Okie Noodling* and founder of the annual contest, remarked on this type of fraud in an article in *Gastronomica*. "Every year," he said, "somebody accuses somebody of cheating, and I'll be like, 'Well, he has to sleep with himself.'"

As we moved from hole to hole all afternoon, it was interesting to watch the Bivins family. They were joking and wrassling, sometimes hopping on one another's backs or towing each other around. With all the verses from scripture on their website and shout-outs to the Lord, I was expecting a more Evangelistic experience, but Skipper was using just as many four-letter words as I was.

Another interesting observation was that a lot of touching goes on when noodling. To write that there's a "homosocial" factor, however, misses the point. It doesn't matter what gender you are. When you're trying to block all exits from a catfish hole, hands brush butts and nuts and boobs. People cram their shoulders together, sit in each others' laps, and hug each other for stability. There's no shame at all, and modesty is nonexistent, because that's what you have to do to get a fish.

But we weren't getting a fish. We were getting skunked. So we decided to head back, which took almost two hours. It was more swimming than I'd done since I was a kid, and we all had super-pruney skin.

It was six o'clock when we got back to the creek by the put-in spot, and now there were fishermen lining the banks. Some were fishing with rod and reel (otherwise known as "sissy fishing," according to Skipper), but some were grabbling the spots we'd already checked.

Christian went up the creek to check out some holes, and the next thing I knew JoAnn said he had one. Skipper and I ran over. Christian was sitting down with his legs stuck under some roots in the bank.

"It's on my foot," he said, "and there's another one in here."

Skipper dove down and stringered the fish (another beautiful one-eyed blue, also about twenty pounds), then sat me down on Christian's lap. I slipped in and felt the cat. It was wiggling right against my calf and wedged into the far corner of the den facing away from me. I couldn't reach it with my arm or even a stick, and I tried everything I could to get my toes in front of its face to turn it around. I tried for twenty minutes, knowing that if we had a shovel, we could have just dug a foot down through the bank and hauled it right out of there.

Skipper then told me to clear some mud from under my butt. This allowed me to drop down another couple inches and slide my foot forward another inch. That was all I needed. I got my toes in front of the fish and turned it around.

It immediately shot for the opening, which, of course, was blocked by me. Reaching down, I got ahold of its head, and my instincts knew what to do. I put one hand right in its mouth, and when it bit down I slid my other hand in and grabbed the other jaw. I then pulled it out without a stringer, because I knew it was small. That little sucker, also a blue, weighed only two pounds. I could hardly believe it was sexually mature enough to be in there with a fish eighteen pounds heavier, but there it was in my hands.

Skipper noodled a random carp out of nowhere, then told Christian to work the bank while he went across to the opposite side. I guess Skipper felt I knew enough now to go off on my own, because he told me to work Christian's bank going the other way.

Noodling is dangerous, and it's not advisable to go solo. People usually work in teams, watch each other's backs, and build strong bonds. The spirit of cooperation is always involved. But every year people drown. I even saw Skipper snag his sock on a lost rusty trotline hook—and now I was on my own.

To make things even more terrifying, I discovered a den beneath a snag. I yelled to Christian, who wasn't too far away, and he came over and told me to check it out. So suddenly I was sticking my legs into unfamiliar territory, and Skipper was almost two hundred yards away. The fear hit me, but I couldn't chicken out. I did it reluctantly and was glad to find the hole empty.

Then Skipper called us over. He had discovered another den, and it was in a pretty clear spot where I could operate sitting up next to a dead gar on the shore. I got to work. The fish attacked ferociously, and I got both feet in its mouth. This one was bigger than the others, and it was hard to keep those jaws pried open. It kept trying to shake free, especially when I pulled it into the tunnel and Skipper went in with the stringer. I held on, though, and pulled it out thrashing like a maniac: a fat, dark blue cat, just upward of twenty pounds.

This one I decided to keep, and if we caught a bigger one the next day, so much the better. We put it in a plastic swimming pool in the back of Skipper's truck and followed him along a hot, paved country road swarming with black-brown tarantulas. When we got to the Redneck Riviera, the lodge where we were staying, we put the big cat in a cattle trough filled with well water and hooked up a pump.

Over the course of that night, I dragged my extremely sun-fried back and shoulders out of bed twice and with sore legs went out to check that tank and make sure the filter hadn't clogged with algae, depleting the tank of oxygen.

By 7:00 a.m., I was redder than a hobo's nose. I considered not going out, because I already had my fish. But since we'd be heading to the river that morning, there was a possibility I could catch an even bigger one. Not only that; I hadn't noodled a flathead yet, so it made sense to try again.

Skipper and Christian arrived at eight and we took off for the river, which was running cold with salinity. Yep, that stream was salt water, right in the middle of the USA, thanks to running through various salt deposits. Still, it was low-level salinity, which flatheads can take.

This time I was wearing a shirt and cap. I had also applied sunscreen an hour before entering the water, whereas the day before I'd done it right before going in.

We took off downstream and met two old boys in an airboat fishing for channel cats. Skipper and one of them got talking, and it didn't take long before they hit on the subject of a recent oil spill: a pipeline had burst in this area just like on my lake back in Arkansas and in other places all over the world. This particular spill, however, resulted in a massive fishkill.

"There must've been a thousand fish on this shore, bloating in the sun," Skipper said. "There were thirty-pounders, forty-pounders, fifty-pounders everywhere."

"The state said it was an infestation of blue algae," the older man replied. He had also seen the fishkill.

"That's a bunch of bull," Skipper shot back. "It was the oil. The big fish were the first to go."

This got them talking about how they'd fished this river all their lives, and how the fishing quality just wasn't what it used to be. There used to be loads of big ones all up and down that bank, and sixty- and seventy-pounders in that hole over there, but now things were different. That was the basic message.

The airboat guys left and we got back to working the shore. Skipper was checking under logs and snags and Christian and I were flanking him. And despite the fact that the fishing wasn't up to snuff, we kept stepping on random cats and spooking carp brushing up against us.

Then we met a cottonmouth, which surprised Skipper, because it was a bit colder out than snakes usually like. This made Skipper nervous, and we all went into an elevated serpent-watching mode. Skipper got a forked stick, snuck up on that moccasin, and pinned it to the sand. Christian got a club-sized piece of driftwood and beat it to death.

Ten minutes later, we found a log half-buried in the river sand with an opening beneath it. Skipper blocked the hole and sent me upstream

FIG. 22. Skipper, Spitzer, Christian, and sixty pounds of flathead cats. Photo by RJB Photo.

to check for another entrance, which I immediately found. It was a way bigger opening, so Christian switched places with his father, and then Skipper slipped into the bigger hole, and I slipped in in front of him.

In no time at all I felt the cat. It was a big one and it wanted out. It swam right into my crotch, and I immediately got a grip on its head.

"Wrap your legs around it," Skipper said.

I did that, then worked my fingers down to its mouth. It wasn't hard at all. I grasped the top jaw with one hand, got the lower jaw with the other, and pried them apart. That fish was totally in my control. I held it as Skipper went under and ran the stringer straight through its underjaw flesh and out of its mouth, then handed it off to me. I wound the un-fish end of the stringer around my wrist, and then I felt another fish in the hole. It was also pretty dang big.

I yanked out the first fish, and it thrashed like a shark attack, a beautiful, golden flatty weighing no less than thirty pounds. She was preggie and fat and full of roe, but we still had another cat to go.

For a minute or so the second fish swam back and forth between Christian and me, not opting to bite my feet. Ultimately, though, it ended up in the same spot as its mate, and I got both my hands into its mouth. Skipper went down and strung it up, and then there was another eruption. This one was about the same size. In less than five minutes, we had sixty pounds of catfish on the stringer, and the high-fives were going around.

The female weighed a couple more pounds, but we put her back, along with the tens of thousands of eggs she'd soon release. I've read that a typical flathead clutch works out to 2,640 eggs per kilogram of fish, but I've also seen the exact same figure per pound. Similarly, I've read that a female flathead's average production is a hundred thousand eggs, a figure that other sources cite as the max. If anything, the confusion that exists over not having an officially recognized figure for egg generation points to the fact that there are still opportunities for serious research on this species.

Anyhow, now that I had my scuffed and bloody tournament fish with shredded fins (from mating or fighting or both), it was time to head back to the ranch, let the blue cat go, and make our way to the contest.

Burning fingers bleeding, we drove north to Paul's Valley, my three-and-a-half-foot cat chilling out in the tub in back. I'd taken a 150-gallon cattle stock tank and had rigged up a faucet connected to a drainage hose. I'd also made a waterproof plywood lid, which was sealed tight with ratchet straps. The tub had an opening for ventilation on top and two holes drilled in the lid with oxygen tubes going through them; one connected to a battery-powered bubbler, the other hooked up to a 150-gallon aquarium aerator running off the converter in my cigarette lighter. We were in my Jeep Grand Cherokee, and the AC was keeping us and the fish cool.

We were the very first of the 113 registered contestants to arrive at the 15th Annual Okie Noodling Tournament as well as the only contestant vehicle that wasn't a pickup truck. The security guards and parking lot guys were eager to see the fish, and they directed me to the unloading area, where the anticipation was palpable. It was about two o'clock in the afternoon, and people were hungry to see a big cat.

I got it out of the tub and slung it over my shoulder. Escorts whizzed me toward the stage, and there were cell-phone cameras held aloft everywhere. I kept stopping for photos, and then some noodling queen with plastic hillbilly teeth insisted on getting a shot of herself kissing my fish.

Then I heard my name announced on a loudspeaker along with the words "from Conway, Arkansas!" I turned the corner. Suddenly I was up on stage, and there were hundreds of people cheering for me and my fish, and hundreds more running for the band shell. They were hopping up and down, pumping fists in the air, and screaming as if I was the Beatles, circa '64. It was such a shocking reception that my jaw actually dropped. Their excitement pumped me up, and the electricity in the air was like nothing I'd ever experienced before and will probably never experience again.

The judges tagged the fish with a big red #1 on a pectoral fin, then took it to the scale. Though I weighed this fish on my own scale at twenty-nine pounds, they weighed it in at 28.5, then led me over to the photo area. The crowd continued going wild, and when I hoisted that fish over my head, the audience exploded again.

I then made my way to the demonstration tank, where the back slaps and fist bumps were enthusiastic and sincere. Kids wanted to know where I had caught the fish and reporters were sticking microphones in my face. It was usually the other way around, but not today. At this point, I was #1! I was the winner—posing with my champion flatty, strangers flinging their arms around me just to get into the shot.

I gave my fish to the guy in charge of the tank and he lowered it in. Kids ran up and pressed their faces to the glass, *oooing* and *awwing* and checking it out. Their glee was totally intense. This was what they'd come to see.

Then two more guys rolled in and unloaded two little cats, no bigger than six pounds each. One of them had won the prize for smallest fish last year, and that's what they were going for again. Their fish went in with mine, and for the next two hours, my fish ruled that tank. It was the giant dominating cat—which hundreds of kids saw and remember and even dream about to this day.

Rob and I then made the rounds. We bought some Okie Noodling shirts and went over to the Bare Knuckle Babe booth, where buxom attendants in tank tops and Daisy Dukes and cowboy boots were signing copies of a calendar. Each month featured a bikini-clad gal and a completely naked sexy cat.

There were food stands as well, and beer and merchandise and all sorts of county fair stuff like bouncy castles and bull rides and dunk tanks galore. But the main attraction, at least for the kids, was the flathead I had noodled with my bare bleeding hands.

Around four o'clock more fish started coming in, and since Rob and I were with the media (thanks to my trusty homemade "PRESS" badge), we were granted access to the cordoned-off VIP area. From this vantage point, we could take pictures of the contestants unloading their cats and parading them up to the stage. I could also jot down the necessary details, take notes, and interview the noodlers.

The categories were Natural (for traditional hand-fishing), Scuba (taken by spear gun), Smallest Fish, Women's Fish, Under 18, and Big Catch (for the two combined biggest fish in this tournament and the Lake Tawakoni Noodling Contest in Texas). A line of trucks was waiting to unload.

Celebrity noodler Scooter Bivins pulled up and helped his son unload a 51-pound monster, followed by Jessie Dalton with a 36.2-pounder, and Levi and Toby Farris with a couple of 40-pounders. They were followed by another celebrity noodler, Marion Kincaid from *Mudcats*, who brought in a forty-something-pounder. His buddy had one equally as large.

FIG. 23. Scooter Bivins and son. Photo by Mark Spitzer.

After weighing in, some of the fish went into the demonstration tank, but about half of the noodlers took their catches back to the tubs in their trucks. These tanks ranged from cattle troughs to modified poly septic tanks to converted refrigerators, most of them rigged with oxygen pumps and cooling devices.

A young woman named Ashley brought in a 40-pounder and then came a fellow dragging a 47.6-pound flathead on the pavement. A twelve-year-old brought in a 16-pound cat, and a sixteen-year-old followed with a 38.38-pounder. Then a ten-year-old entered the first and only channel cat.

As all this was going on, various noodlers were getting into the demonstration tank and showing how it's done. Scooter and Marion got in and children were chosen by the luck of the draw to noodle with them.

There was also a kids' catfish-eating contest, which conveniently occurred when no catfish were coming in. They had to eat everything on their plates, then show the judges that they didn't have anything in their mouths.

Skipper and JoAnn's daughter Heather, one of the Bare Knuckle Babes, was also on hand and getting a lot of attention. A television crew followed her around, filming a segment for an outdoors show. At one point she was showing the show's host how to pick up a catfish by the mouth. She hoisted a nice forty-pounder out of a tub, and the host tried to follow suit. But when that catfish bit down, he flipped out and threw it back, then went around nursing his wounded hand. He was the only person I saw all day complaining about the pain that comes with noodling.

When the trucks started queuing again, the focus went back to the main stage. Catfish came in weighing 56.54 pounds, 58.24 pounds, 22.92 pounds, 22.48 pounds, 26.5 pounds, and 28.7. That was when the Millsap Clan arrived and made a show of force. The preceding year's champion Lucy Millsap couldn't make it, and her mother was in the lead, trying to juggle a 62-pound fatty, which she fumbled twice in the parking lot. She was followed by Pa Millsap, hoisting another monster cat, his youngest son Bubba III hanging onto the tail. Bubba I and Bubba II also had lunker cats. It was rumored that Ma Millsap had noodled in her daughter's place.

More fish came in, including a 69.9-pound lunker. That one was caught by Ramey Webb, who was the son of Gary Webb, the "Grandfather of Hand-Fishing in Missouri." Gary is a member of Noodlers Anonymous, which had worked to legalize the sport in Missouri. A Texan contestant brought in one that weighed 59.8 pounds, Ted Strickland weighed one in at 62.88, a big fat female cat weighing 55.28 was hoisted high, and then a family called Team Bite Me brought in four catfish for a grand total of nearly 200 pounds.

There was also a lot of blood on stage. I saw a thirteen-year-old kid try to get a hefty flatty out of a tub, and it shredded his fingers and nearly twisted his wrist off. He was bleeding buckets. The crowd, however, cheered his pain away.

Two bare-knuckled babes from the calendar booth then brought a

FIG. 24. Ma Millsap with champion fish. Photo by Mark Spitzer.

50-pounder to the stage together. There was a lot of leg and a lot of cleavage, and the crowd went nuts. But what the audience appreciated even more was a blonde-haired little girl, not much more than three years old, who struggled to the stage with a 16.25-pound flathead. Whereas many suspected that a toddler barely able to hold a fish could have hogged that cat from its hole, everyone was willing to suspend their suspicion because of the cuteness factor.

Team Katt Daddy then arrived with several members and several fish ranging from 36 to 54 pounds, but the *Mudcats* star by this name was nowhere to be seen. His partner Dennis "Copperhead" Williams was, though, his bald head shining in the sun. In the end Brad Beesley, who

FIG. 25. Youngest participant. Photo by Mark Spitzer.

started this whole phenomenon fifteen years ago, made a speech about how the event had evolved from having an audience of two hundred in a barbecue shack to attracting ten to fifteen thousand people each year.

This year they were honoring Gary Webb with a lifetime achievement award. Gary took the stage with some help from Marion, who took the mic and talked about Gary's failing health and the fact that he'd been active in popularizing noodling. Gary's son Ramey then honored his father further by claiming the $1,500 prize for Biggest Fish. Ma Millsap scored the $200 prize for Top Female Noodler, which I had to investigate, since some were saying that she wasn't even registered. When I called the woman in charge of tourism at City Hall a few days later, she assured me such talk was just gossip and the Millsaps were the "most politest" noodling family she'd ever met.

Sellor Lane won the $200 Youth award with his 56.54-pound catfish, and Tim Suchy took home the $400 Scuba division prize for his 62.88-pound flathead. Bobby Gutherless Anderson's 3.26-pound channel reigned victorious for the Smallest Fish award. Pa Millsap won the $1,000 Big Catch prize, and Bubba II placed third in the Natural division.

But Rob and I we were too burned out to hang out anymore. Forgoing the live band and crowning of the Noodling Queen, we lit off for Arkansas.

In the car I felt a strange combination of adrenaline and being bummed. Right before we left, I'd gone over to say goodbye to my fish and was slapped in the face by what I saw. Oblivious children were diving down and grabbing it, then laughing as they lifted it up to show off, their grubby little hands pressing into its guts. That's what often kills big fish, which are used to zero gravity: damage to internal organs from being manhandled. Not only that, but kids were stepping on my catfish's head as they tried to get to other fish.

A gentle giant, he'd come in scuffed and bloody, resigned to his fate, and now I could see that resignation even more in his eyes. My fish knew he was a goner, and I knew I was responsible for everything he was feeling now.

That's when I saw the underbelly of noodling, which takes more super-sized cats out of the system than rod and reel could ever hope to equal. That belly come floating by, pale and distended, on one of the smaller cats that the second and third guys had brought in. That cat was twirling around stiff and dead, noodled to death by fascinated kids.

I tried to articulate what I thought. Having bloodied myself in the name of hand-fishing, I could now make a more experienced judgment call, and there was something about the "sport" that didn't sit right with me. Something about breaking into their homes, which were designed specifically for reproduction, then yanking them into our cruel world. Something about ending up with more questions than I started with.

Questions like: What happens to all those catfish that the noodlers take back to their trucks? And what happens to fish in the demonstration tank, which are reportedly eaten—even though it's well known that big cats are full of toxins like mercury, lead, PCBs, and insecticides? And could overfishing through noodling lend to further weakening of an already compromised species?

Because what Skipper and the old boy he spoke to had noted about fishing going down in their area, that's happening everywhere. It's what happened with alligator gar throughout their range, and we're still trying to recover from that. It's why there are no twenty-foot white sturgeon any longer. And it's why paddlefish have to be stocked for the fisheries to exist. That's what I've been researching, that's what I've been writing about, and the fact is that when it comes to flathead cats, there are no hundred-pounders any more.

These days, noodling is legal in some form or another in at least a dozen states, and there are now more noodling competitions than in any time before, and they're increasing exponentially. At the tournament I received flyers for two other Oklahoma noodling contests, and I heard about a couple more before I left the state. There are competitions in Texas, Kentucky, Tennessee, Arkansas, and Mississippi—and those are just the legal ones. As for illegal competitions, noodling happens all over the country as an outlaw sport, so it's hard to know how many people are doing it, but there are estimates in the tens of thousands, though hundreds of thousands might be taking part. And while all this is going on, fueled by constant TV shows, online videos, and movies that hype up the noodling craze, it's indisputably true that "The unprecedented use of fresh water has led to declining populations of many aquatic species, particularly 'megafishes' which are disappearing at an alarming rate. It's now a race against the clock to protect and document the aquatic life in these water systems." That's what Zeb Hogan's *Megafishes Project* website states is its mission, and that's why I write these books. These observations come from real knowledge from documenting populations in serious decline. Especially the big ones, for which reproduction is highly complex.

Texas Parks and Wildlife has been surveying catfish populations in order to assess the consequences of legalized hand-fishing, and according to the *Houston Chronicle*, the "results are in the noodlers' favor." The exploitation rate is "only 5%, which . . . shows the population is sustainable."

But what are we sustaining? We're sustaining crippled populations, in which apex predators only grow half as huge as they used to get. And with climate change and oil spills becoming more unpredictable, I can't help wondering if "sustainable" numbers can remain so sustainable.

We don't know. We can't know. All we can do is argue or take action. In the meantime, we're taking a chance on one of the coolest fish we've ever known. If we want to keep flatheads around that can surpass 150 pounds like they used to do in the 1800s, we had better do something fast.

But rather than pick sides, here's what I propose: Instead of maintaining the status quo (which is actually small potatoes, when 70-pounders could be 170-pounders), let's take 10 percent of the largest ones from all catfishing competitions and put them in preserves like they have for wels catfish in Catalonia's Ebre Delta National Park in Spain and Russia's Astrakhanky State Nature Reserve. Mingo Swamp in Missouri has a successful program for alligator gar restoration, which could also serve as a working model. Then let's let our cats get as huge as they can, so that when the playing field is leveled, we can allow a limited number of noodlers and rod 'n' reelers into these areas on a lottery system to catch and release monster flatheads the way God meant them to be: ginormous, ferocious, and pound for pound, equal in size to us. Then let's see who's tougher: man or fish.

This is my challenge to the noodling community, which has no fear of hundred-pounders. This is also my challenge to any tourist economy promoters savvy and progressive enough to capitalize on a truly sustainable, highly specialized trophy-fish industry. It's a win-win situation. The environmentalists get to see some amazing fish get protected, and the proudly self-proclaimed rednecks will be assured that their grandchildren can wrestle the full-sized fatties their granddaddies used to tackle in hand-to-hand combat. Because what it all boils down to this: if we've got the will and the huevos to let our fish reach their full potential for growth, then maybe we can reach our own.

8

Muskie Hunting in Minnesota

An Education in "the Fish of Ten Thousand Casts"

They're there, they're rare, they're nearly impossible to catch, and they're one of the most sought after trophy fish on this continent. As the grandpappy of the pike family, sometimes weighing seventy pounds, this fish is seen as beautiful, but it's also a fantastic living grotesque. Hence the name muskellunge, which comes from a corruption of French and Anishinaabe (the Chippewa language) and basically translates as "big old ugly long-ass pike with a deformed head." These qualities are supported by a reputation as a mythical, monstrous wolf of the water known for gulping down ducks and chomping off toes. So how could I not go after this fish?

In the United States, true native muskie range as far west as eastern Iowa, but they've been introduced into Arkansas, Arizona, Colorado, Nebraska, Missouri, Oklahoma, Texas, and both Dakotas. I decided, however, to shoot for my home state, Minnesota, where muskie have been stocked, especially around the Twin Cities area, and they've supplemented the indigenous populations. It was a fish I had never caught before or even tried to target, but when July came along, it was time.

My schooling began on Leech Lake, perhaps the most famous muskie lake in the world as well as one that produces a huge, healthy, long-living strain that's in demand by other states for its hardy genetics. After cramming my head full of articles and research, I hired two guides out of the town of Walker, not too far from the source of the Mississippi River, which flows north of the lake's west side then cuts south in the shape of a question mark. So technically, Leech Lake is east of the Mississippi; but it's far enough west to fall within the parameters of what I've established as the West for the purposes of this book.

My first guide was Mark Christianson, an extremely tanned walleye tournament champ who'd been guiding in the area for twenty-eight years. He runs a resort on Agency Bay, where I met him at 8:00 a.m. and noticed two things right off the bat. First, he frequently laughed to himself at random thoughts flashing through his head—a quirky personality trait that I immediately appreciated, whether he shared those thoughts or not. And second, he had that whimsical northern Minnesota accent that I always find amusing. Mark took me out to the cabbage weed growing eight feet beneath the surface, and that was where we started casting—because muskie guides don't just sit there. They cast just as much as you, because they want to land a lunker too.

The water was seventy degrees, and I was using a bright orange double bucktail spinner and keeping it right beneath the surface. Mark was using a ten-inch tangerine plastic jerkbait with black perchy stripes. We both had sturdy seven-foot casting rods equipped with Ambassadeur 6500 baitcasting reels strung up with 50-pound braided test and 120-pound steel leaders, and he showed me the twitching technique. All it took was a slight downward flick of the rod's tip every few cranks, and that lure would twerk like an injured fish.

Then it happened, just like that. Within half an hour of hitting the water, Mark connected with a three-and-a-half-foot muskie. It leapt four feet into the air (a sure sign it wasn't a northern pike), it had a long white underbelly, and it was thrashing all silvery—an image that burned itself into every remaining brain cell in my head as the fish slapped back into the lake.

That muskie then made a hard, fast run away from the boat, but Mark horsed it over and we got a better look at it. The fish was snagged in the side, which made fighting it a delicate procedure. If it turned a certain

FIG. 26. Mark Christianson and muskie. Photo by Mark Spitzer.

way or got any slack, that barb could pop out, so he had to keep the line tight and wear it out before it shook the hook.

Mark fought it for five minutes as I shot back and forth from rail to rail with the oversized landing net, which would also demand some precision attention. If the fish didn't go in headfirst and perfectly, if it hit the rim and flinched, it could snap and unhook itself. And that muskie—being a species with highly acute eyesight—I saw it see that net, and I saw that it didn't like what it saw.

It lit off on another run, but when Mark brought it back, it was too beat to flee. He led it in, I scooped it up, and the moment it hit the deck, the hook popped out.

The muskie was streaming blood from between its eyes where a triangular chunk of meat had been ripped from its head and was hanging by a strip of skin. We figured it had missed the lure and been hooked in the face, and then the instant that it tore loose, it snagged itself again.

Mark measured the fish at forty-two inches, and we estimated it to be twenty-something pounds. Whereas muskie used to be measured by the pound, as are most sport fish, they're mostly measured in inches now. The biggest ones are in the fifties, but the record ones are in the sixties. Six-footers have been recorded, and at that point, they're about equal in pounds and in inches.

As Mark posed with the fish, I took a closer look. Those flaring gills were louvered in a sharky way, and the muskie was chromy on the sides with oblong spots. Mark called it "a silver," though technically it was a spotted. The other two subspecies are barred and Chautauqua, the latter being an eastern fish. The tiger muskie, on the other hand, is a hybrid with a northern pike that sometimes occurs naturally in the wild, but for the most part, they're produced en masse and stocked by state agencies.

Since catch and release is the norm, Mark put it back in the water. He held it for a while as it gained its bearings, but it wasn't doing very well. It was still bleeding, and it was tilting toward a belly-up position. And when Mark finally let it go, it rolled, gasping from its heaving breast.

Seeing that great fish struggling for its life was definitely a messed-up sight. When a fish floats like that, it's pretty much toast, so Mark grabbed it by the tail. But when he turned it over to cradle it, it shook off its daze and dove for the weeds.

The rest of the day was anticlimactic, but I learned a lot. Like how to adjust the casting dial on the reel properly, and how to jerk the jerkbait. I also tried out a bunch of lures, like a super-sized jake that swished from side to side, and an extra-large double cowgirl with two chromatic blades that rotate in opposite directions, followed by a foot of black and silver tinsel covering two treble hooks. It flashed like a saber as it sliced through the water, sending out a sonic vibration that I thought nary a red-blooded muskie could refuse.

But they did. At least three or four times we saw a thick brown back follow our lures in, then turn away. Those muskies were about the same size as the one Mark caught, and I got a hit off a single one twice, because after it struck the first time then let go, it lurched for the lure again. A split second later it struck a second time and caused a minor disruption on the surface, but not enough to seal the deal.

By the end of the day Mark had caught two northerns, and I caught one, not much larger than sixteen inches. It was a gorgeous, stripy olive-green fish.

When we pulled up to Mark's dock, the question put to us was whether we'd caught a muskie, and the answer, of course, was yes. Still, I didn't feel as if that fish was *ours*, even though Mark was in my employment, and I had netted it.

"I guess I could frame it like *we* caught it," I told Mark, but I just didn't feel that was legit. I still had 9,600 casts to go, according to the standard equation, and I still had another day on the lake. That's what I figured as I shook Mark's hand, and he chuckled to himself just as much as to me.

My second guide was Jeff Woodruff, a white-whiskered veteran of the lake who'd been guiding since '71. On the phone he promised me stories, and that's what I got immediately, starting with "the Muskie Rampage of 1955." For some strange reason, Jeff explained, a hundred muskies were landed on that day. They were bringing them in in wheelbarrows because the fish had gone berserk, biting like crazy, and to this day no one knows why.

We started with topwater lures with rotating tails that kicked up an audible wake, sounding like a puttering duckling. The rods and reels were pretty much the same as those I'd used the day before, but Jeff's spools were equipped with 36-pound braided line and 124-pound steel leaders. Jeff recommended pulling the lures in a figure eight, the rod tip just above the water, before removing the lure from the water, just in case a muskellunge lunged at the last second.

After an hour I switched to a spinner called booty call and Jeff tried a stud finder. I liked the way they moved through the water, but unlike the day before, the fish just weren't following, and they certainly weren't taking the bait.

That's the way it went through the day. We tried a bunch of different spots, casting for seven hours straight, constantly switching lures. It was the exact opposite of the Muskie Rampage of '55.

But like my day on the lake with Mark, I learned a lot from working with Jeff. He showed me how to make my own leaders, and toward the end of the trip, when I was on the verge of napping out, he showed me how to troll for muskie. We went up and down South Walker Bay pulling fourteen-inch swimbaits that dove to about sixteen feet, where the big ones were showing up on the depth finder. Still, it just wasn't happening.

But I was not disappointed. Since I'd picked one of the most difficult fish in the world to catch, it was reasonable to expect to get skunked for years. Some people fish for muskie all their lives and never get one, so why should I think my experience would be any different? In essence, the odyssey had just begun.

Given the complexities of this extremely elusive fish, I decided to relax my expectations by changing my approach from my usual mode. I usually shoot for just one fish of any size, but with this fish, I figured it would make more sense to allow whatever happens to happen then frame the narrative as a learning experience. With this in mind, I decided that my next step should be either to invest in my own muskie gear or hire another guide who had the gear, which would raise my odds of bagging a muskellunge. So I did both.

My original plan had been to hunt for muskies in the rivers with a family friend named Gabe Schubert, who's built a regional reputation as an accomplished muskie whisperer. He recently guided a client to the state record muskie: a fifty-seven-incher. But to make the record official, the fish would have had to be killed and weighed on a state-certified scale. That option was declined, and the muskie was released.

Gabe's angle is fly fishing. Back in December he had shown me his award-winning flies, which were the most incredible lures I'd ever seen. They were handmade from shiny, elegant feathers, all of them were at least a foot long, and they had even been featured in shows at local art galleries. Not being a very skilled fly fisherman, though, we decided that I should bring my heavy-duty gator gar gear up and fish with live bait.

A few months after that I was waiting in an auto repair shop for a new water pump to be installed on my Jeep when I picked up the May 2014 issue of *Field & Stream*. I started paging through it, and there was Gabe, tying flies. They did a whole feature on his muskie expertise, leaving me even more stoked to fish with him.

After my Jeep was repaired I made off with that magazine as well as another I'd found in that waiting room. The June issue of *Field & Stream* featured another article on muskie. The piece was entitled "I, Muskie Hunter." The editors had asked a Minnesota muskie guide named Josh Stevenson to keep a journal for a year and had published some of his most colorful excerpts. I read about how he had led a client to a super-rare forty-six-inch albino that made major waves in the muskie world, and I read about how he had met his idol, the lead singer from Metallica. Other excerpts included getting a finger totally skewered by a treble hook and landing his personal best fifty-six-inch fish. It was a highly entertaining piece, and it gave some insight into a professional whose life was dedicated to the culture and catching of muskellunge. Unfortunately, he guided up by Lake Mille Lacs, which is on the east side of the Mississippi.

Or so I thought.

When I reread the article, I saw that in one of the pictures Josh was wearing a t-shirt that said "Blue Ribbon Bait and Tackle." I had just contacted this specialized tackle shop near my mother's home to find out about their occasional jumbo suckers, which I had planned to stock up on.

But when I'd arrived in Minnesota to fish with Gabe, I had to give up on the live bait idea, because the rivers were so flooded that he told me our chances were nil. That's why I had gone to Leech Lake.

The article said Josh was a tackle store owner as well as a guide who

FIG. 27. Minnesota state record tiger muskie. Photo by Mark Spitzer.

ran a service called Mighty Musky. And since some excerpts from his journal sported the dateline "Oakdale MN," I put two and two together. Josh was the owner of the very tackle store I'd already contacted, and he was just down the road from me.

The next thing you know, I was in his shop and checking out the stripy mount of his Minnesota state record tiger muskie. It weighed thirty-nine pounds, and it was a whopper.

Josh came in with his toddler daughter, I hired him to take me out in a week, and in the meantime I bought some trolling gear. This gear included a ten-inch jake, a metallic-gold twelve-inch super stalker, an eight-inch perch-colored shallow raider, and a rainbow-colored shallow diver with a hinged "action tail." I made sure that all these lures had orange on them, because that was the color muskies had been hitting on at Leech Lake. I also got some 150-pound mono-leaders, some 100-pound black steel leaders, and a 100-pound Knot2Kinky titanium leader. The tackle cost over $120, but so what? As usual, the plan was to write it off along with the guides, gas, food, and motel expenses I constantly incur when researching fish.

For the next two weeks I went trolling and casting all over the state. I didn't see any muskies, but I caught plenty of northerns along the way, sometimes up to seven per day, and they were always a blast to fight, especially when my nine-year-old nephew netted them. The lure that worked best for me was a bright yellow Mepps muskie killer spinner, which buzzed through the water and could always be seen. I preferred spinners over crankbaits for the constant buzz you can always feel vibing through the water, and I fed the extended family several times, mostly with super-bony grilled fillets topped with a caper-dill cream sauce. The most valuable thing I learned, though, while catching pike in pursuit of muskie, was how to crank back extremely hard after the strike, setting the hook—a lesson I intended to apply to the first muskie I got on my line.

When I finally got out on the undisclosed metro-area lake with Josh, it was 6:00 a.m., the sun just rising through the misty reeds. We shot to the spot on his sparkly Skeeter powered by a 300-horsepower Yamaha. Josh was also equipped with two state-of-the-art Humminbird fish finders, one for him and one for me. This time I was using a Shimano 300-model baitcasting reel spooled with eighty-pound braid and a hundred-pound fluorocarbon leader on an eight-foot-six Tooth Tamer rod. The casting knob was a lot easier to access and turn on this reel than on any of the Abu Garcias, and the ultra-strong plastic leader wouldn't kink up like the steel ones after a few hours of casting.

I was on the bow and Josh was in the stern, and we were shooting for a rock that he said the fish liked to gather around. That was when I saw two black-cherry-colored fins stirring around on the surface; one was the dorsal and the other the tail. It was a three-foot-plus muskie feeding just twenty yards in front of me, so I cast a black bucktail over there and reeled it through the weeds. It came humming in with no muskie behind. At least, that's what I thought until the fish came busting up from the black water, snapping at the spinner. And after it missed, it snapped again.

I pulled the bucktail out, but Josh told me to get my pole back in the water and swirl it around in a circle. I did that, and he told me to get the tip in deeper and not to stop—for about a minute straight. It didn't work.

"Aww man!" Josh said, excited by the strike but bummed that I'd missed. "We gotta teach you the figure eight."

He showed me the L-maneuver first, which involves totally submerging the rod tip and making a quick, sharp, ninety-degree turn with the lure, then zipping it along next to the boat to ensure that if anything is down there it will have two seconds more to strike. Josh then demonstrated a much more involved underwater figure eight compared to what I'd done on Leech Lake with my rod tip above the water. His technique was to reel all the way up to the leader and plunge the rod tip about a foot beneath the surface and keep it going, which I practiced all day long and got pretty good at.

We moved on to another spot, and an hour later another muskie followed my bucktail in. I just happened to glance down, and there it was right next to the boat. With the sun higher in the sky and the water shimmering greenishly, it looked like a four-foot-long, pine-green log of a fish just casually hovering there. It was only a few feet away from me and every detail was totally defined, down to its eyeballs, which rotated up toward mine. When our eyes met, it took off.

Since this fish had definitely been spooked, my instinct was to pull out and give up, but Josh told me do the figure eight again, because muskies don't frighten as easily as other fish, and sometimes they come back. I did that for a bit, but it was gone.

"Man!" Josh said. "That's two follows and one strike, and it's not even eight o'clock."

Josh, meanwhile, was casting a bulbous loon-colored topwater lure that sputtered up a bubbly sound. It was oddly shaped, like a cartoon-looking neutron bomb, and he could chuck it nearly seventy yards. It wasn't attracting as much attention as my bucktail, but thirty minutes later he got a follow. It was another four-footer, this one appearing like a fat brown duck-billed cylinder. It also saw us and shot off.

By nine in the morning, I officially had the Fever. It didn't matter that I'd had too little sleep the night before. My life was now changed, and I'd damn well cast all day, maybe for the rest of my life. No other fish existed in the world, not even gar.

Since I wanted to learn as much as I could, Josh switched my spinner to a silver-blue showgirl, little sister of the cowgirl. He also hooked me up with a Shimano Curado 300DSV reel, a type I'd never tried before.

FIG. 28. Chomped northern pike. Photo by Josh Stevenson.

It's like any standard baitcaster, but it has a fendery-looking extension up front that makes the whole shape seem aerodynamic and enclosed. Josh showed me how to open up the side panel and adjust the six brakes to make it tighter or looser when casting, and he also oiled it under the casting knob and along the tracks, which is something I'd never done with any of my reels and should have learned years ago. Anyhow, I took to that reel, and it took to me. We had a love affair, and before the day was over Josh sold it to me.

Around noon he got another follow, which surprised us both, since we'd passed the prime time for activity, and according to Josh, we were now defying the odds. This muskie was about forty-two inches long, and it was curious about the foot-long yellow twitch-bait Josh was jerking just under the surface. This muskellunge was lazy, though, and when it saw the boat it faded away.

Then suddenly WHAM!—a fish hit my line and dove into the weeds.

My rod bowed and I set the hook. When I brought it in splashing and thrashing, Josh scooped it up with the net. It was a two-foot northern, and to our surprise, it had a freshly bleeding chomp mark on its side. A monster muskie had done the deed not more than a few hours before, and as the fish stared up at us, I could see in its pikey eyes that this was the worst day of its life.

Another thing I learned from Josh that I hadn't known before was how to hold a pike or muskie properly. Rather than sticking my fingers in through the delicate red feathery frills, he told me to put them behind the gill plate and above the first fringy layer, which made a lot of sense. That way I'd be supporting the fish in a place that could take it, rather than crunching up its fragile gillage.

Then I got another hit, a good small pike that shook itself off. After that, two more muskies followed Josh's lure but weren't committed enough to go for it.

At this point, the problem was that I was learning more than I was catching—for which Josh was apologetic. But I didn't care, because my adjusted mission was to glean from his store of knowledge. Basically, I was taking the course Muskie Hunting 101, and I was an eager student.

One of the lessons I learned from Josh was his "blue shirt theory," which is about blending in with the sky. Josh usually wears blue shirts when guiding for muskie, but he'd grabbed a brighter-colored shirt that day while running out the door, and he was worried that a fish might catch a glimpse of him and hesitate. So in the early afternoon when the sun was high, he hunkered down low to be less visible while I was casting. I was wearing a gray t-shirt, which worked well with the overcast, and a couple more followed my lure in.

Of course, we were both wearing polarized sunglasses to see through the water better. As usual, mine had orange lenses, which I like because they make things seem brighter and therefore easier to see.

Had I not been wearing those shades, I never would have seen a sudden three-and-a-half-footer that followed my showgirl in. It hung back about eight feet, close to the surface, and with the early afternoon sun pounding down, it looked like a strangely defined sturgeon, its dark silhouette lit up whitely around the edges to the point that I could see the highly defined rays on its fins.

Having now fished with three guides, I was also learning that spotting a muskie counts. Muskie junkies literally quantify their success on the water by the amount of "follows" they get per day in relation to actually landing a fish. They frame fishing trips with stats like 6 for 1, an attitude I favor. I mean, sometimes I go out just to see the gator gar roll, with no intention of trying to catch one. Because for those who love fish, seeing a lunker can be a thrill in itself that carries its own currency. Essentially, that's what birdwatchers do. Rather than catching the creature, they collect mental images that are rewards in themselves.

Getting a strike, however, is that space between a follow and a fish, which can be just as much of a rush as it is frustrating. That's what happened toward the end of the day. I was back to the bucktail and bringing it in when a big silver side broke right next to the boat. It was a twenty-plus-pounder with white spots, and when it missed I jammed my rod into the drink. The fish instantly torqued down on the lure, totally intent on "smoking it," as the parlance of the culture goes. In the next nanosecond the fish lashed a quart of water into my face and grabbed the spinner. But just as soon as that happened, it got off, leaving me cheering instead of swearing.

By the end of the day we were 7 and 0, but I didn't give a muskie butt. These encounters provided me with something I never expected: there was a new fish in my life, one that was just as electrifying as it was maddening.

Still, I had to give it one more shot, so in mid-August I hooked up with Gabe, the fly-tying muskie whisperer with whom I had originally planned to fish. The river levels were down, and he was driving, a specialized rowboat in tow.

The difference between river muskie and lake muskie, according to

Gabe (whom I'm now paraphrasing), is that the fish living in moving water are more opportunistic. Because water levels fluctuate, causing fish to move around more in river systems, river muskies "work for their living" more than those in lakes, where they tend to stake out feeding zones where food fish hang out for weeks at a time.

We discussed the overall muskellunge fishery, which has been extremely successful in Minnesota and beyond. Thanks to responsible stewardship and attention to stocking and catch and release, these trophy fish are now available to millions of anglers from coast to coast, and because of this, they're thriving just as much as the sport, which has mushroomed.

Native wild strains are inevitably mixing with hatchery fish, which works to homogenize the genetics in general. But that's what's been happening with trout for decades, and that's what has to happen to have such fish rather than none at all.

I asked Gabe what he thought had provoked the Muskie Rampage of '55. I'd also put this question to Josh, who figured it was due to a fluctuation in the populations of cisco, on which muskie feed voraciously. Gabe, though, figured it was something unique about the weather. Perhaps barometric pressure, or some sort of weird moon or peculiar light, or a combination of such factors along with others. Who knows?

We arrived at the undisclosed river, which was shallow and undeveloped, with a rocky bottom. The water was a bright, stained, root-beer color, and with the sun shining down from the triple-blue sky, the visibility was simply awesome. In fact, after ten minutes on the water (Gabe rowing in the middle, me up front) we saw a vivid and unworldly sight in the shimmering current: a four-foot sturgeon just hanging out on the bottom, a lamprey glommed onto its head.

An eagle gave us a flyover, and I noticed there was no net on board. Gabe explained that he lands muskies by hand, because sometimes nets tear up their tails. To bring one in, he rows to shore and gets into the water with them—a concept, I figured, that would be just as interesting to see as it is unusual.

Gabe had brought along three extra-large fly-fishing rods, but I was psyched to try my new futuristic Curado reel I'd bought from Josh on a brand-new eight-foot-six "Extra Extra Heavy" Shimano rod. I also had a bunch of really sweet lures with me, including a double-treble black and nickel cowgirl, a coppery tin-buck bucktail, a two-piece shallow raider crankbait, a rainbow-colored UV hinged-tail swimbait, and two fluorescent muskie-model Mepps spinners. Throughout the day I experimented with all of these, but the lure I kept coming back to, and would use primarily on that river, was a super-huge goldish-bronzy cowgirl with an extra-long customized tail made from Icelandic sheep hair Gabe had tied on, making the whole thing more than sixteen inches long. With that sexy undulating tail, it came through the water like a redhorse sucker in distress.

Within half an hour a big one lit after it. I didn't see the fish, but Gabe said it was a forty-four-inch male.

Half an hour after that I saw the water boil when I slapped that cowgirl down by the shore, and someone else went for it. That muskie shoved the water up from below and came burning in straight for my lure.

But it didn't hit. None of those fish hit. Still, I did get a mild strike another twenty minutes later. All morning long, they kept following in less than a foot of water, close to the shore where springs fed in and water weeds hid smaller fish. I even saw a cute little army-green muskie smiling as it tailed my coppery cowgirl, which was about the same size as the fish. That lure was wreaking havoc with my back, but I wasn't going to let something as commonplace as fatigue get to me.

We came in at 2:45 and hit the road to a place upstream. An outfitter helped shuttle us, and within an hour we were back on the water, floating a six-mile stretch through dark green water with occasional rapids, ospreys soaring above. We got a lot less hits in this spot, but then we came to a creek, and Gabe told me to cast into the middle of it.

And here he came: a big black telephone pole of a muskie focused on the flash. Gabe got a better look and identified it as a male, while I kept my eyes pegged on the cowgirl. I didn't want it to twitch or pause or do anything to make the fish question what it was chasing down— when suddenly it stopped.

I sensed that it sensed us as it vanished back into the shadows. But then Gabe got a glimpse of it heading upstream. He told me exactly where to cast, and I hit that spot. That muskie, however, wasn't about to be fooled again.

"That was one old muskie," Gabe said. He threw in an adjective I can't recall, but the implication was that this fish was so damn ancient and suspicious that it wasn't about to take any guff from the likes of us.

And so we kept floating. And I kept casting. To the point of utter exhaustion.

And that's the story. There's no resolution. Like millions with the Fever, I got my ass kicked by muskellunge. Because that's the nature of this beast.

"Geez," I told Gabe on the ride back, "when I go after a fish, I usually get it eventually. But this fish defeated me."

I was trying to make peace with the realization that my pursuit of muskie had only just begun. Though I didn't accomplish my most selfish goal with this wily leviathan, I had nevertheless accomplished my major objective of getting a muskie-hunting education—the most important lesson being the simple message that if you go out with those who know these fish best, you will see muskie you'll never forget. And if you stick to it, you will experience one of the most epic freshwater fish in existence, one that commands a fierce respect.

In the meantime, I'm still out there casting like a maniac.

9

Vision Questing Gator Gar in the Slick Texas Mud

Garvana Accomplished!

The vision quest idea was really an excuse. I was dead set on catching an alligator gar, and since the Texas Parks and Wildlife Department estimates that "9,200 alligator gar 42 inches long or longer and about 1,400 fish 78 inches or longer" exist in the upper Trinity River, I decided to go for one of them. The spot I'd been thinking of was just below this area, and I'd fished it a few times before, always getting skunked. What I never got skunked on, however, was watching six- and seven-foot behemoths rising and diving in a boldly swirling river bend filled with tons of gator gar. Literally.

The new harvest law of one alligator gar per day enacted in 2009 meant that Texas now had the healthiest, hardiest population of this monsterfish in the world—a sentiment echoed by guides like Dawson Hefner of Texas Megafish Adventures. His website makes the claim, "Texas is the best place for alligator gar fishing in the world"—a truth I had seen with my own eyes. Back when I was working on my first gar book, I caught a 106-pound fatty on the Trinity near Huntsville, and a few years later I assisted Jeremy Wade of *River Monsters* in catching a six-foot-eight alligator gar, also on the Trinity. When working on my

FIG. 29. Spitzer with Jeremy Wade and Trinity River
alligator gar. Courtesy of Icon Films UK.

second gar book, I helped my buddy Minnow Bucket land a three-foot
juvenile from the same river.

So I set off envisioning visions—the main one being me hauling in
a two-hundred-pound, dragon-headed, razor-fanged throwback to the
Jurassic and feeling again that adrenal rush of catching and releasing a
truly beautiful American grotesque. These air-breathing, armor-plated,
prehistoric creatures are the second-largest freshwater fish on the continent. They're capable of surpassing ten feet long, and in this particular
hole, they'd eluded me for six years. So basically, I was shooting to
settle the score.

Season of the Gar was the first book-length overview of the species ever
published in the English language. I sought to debunk misinformation
that had relegated gar to the status of worthless and aggressive trash
fish. Through first-person narratives about going Gonzo for gator gar,
and incorporating science, folklore and history, this book honored gar
as a vital component in the ecosystem and the food chain. I argued for

protection and preservation and made it official that gar do not attack humans, and neither do they eat twice their weight in game fish per day, as rumored.

While working on *Season of the Gar* I was contacted by Jeremy Wade, before the hit series *River Monsters* was ever aired. He invited me to meet him in Texas, bring the bait, and be on the "Alligator Gar" episode of the first season—so that's what I did. He used my research to make a case for the alligator gar, which he ultimately declared not guilty of crimes against humanity. The approach was definitely melo-dramatic, but it worked to convey the messages my book delivered, and because the show and all its reruns reach millions of viewers, awareness of gator gar and their issues increased exponentially. This happened at a time when science was on the rise, and also at a time when new harvesting laws and management plans were kicking in. This overall synergy worked to spread the word that gar are an integral and important part of the environment that shouldn't just be shot in the head for looking ferocious.

My second gar book, *Return of the Gar*, took a closer look at what we've been doing to bring back an imperiled species that has been extirpated throughout its range. In researching this book, I traveled all over the American South, and I also went to Nicaragua, Costa Rica, Thailand, and Mexico to catch gar and interview authorities. In the end I assessed the global gar situation and stressed some more environmental messages, the main one being that we need to keep an eye on our ecosystems and take preemptive action, or else we've got a lot to lose.

Since I began my research as a kid, these gar studies essentially took decades. In the process, gar became a major part of my identity. More important, I feel I've been good for something tangible—which has been incredibly fortunate for me. Not only do I get to make an impact on something worthwhile, I also get to indulge in action-packed fishing adventures all over the world.

But at the moment, heading off on my "vision quest," my gar obsession and I weren't going all over the world. We were going to the next state over, where the biggest, baddest gator gar on the planet were swimming around being huge. And the excitement I was feeling at the prospect of meeting more gar was just as intense as it had been ten years before, when I first went to Texas to fish on the Trinity.

Trailer in tow and twenty grass carp packed in ice, I was bombing down to the Walmart in Athens to pick up a fishing license and supplies. The river was at the exact right level, and I was heading to the most garful hole I'd ever known. But the thing was, it had been raining all day and there was more rain scheduled for that night, which could bring the Trinity up. But what the hell, I figured. It was summer, I had the time, I had the gear, and so what if it rained a bit?

After getting severely stuck in a muddy ditch, I had a couple of hours to get some Texas gator gar research done while waiting for the tow truck. I'd thought I could drive down to the reservoir and catch some more bait to take out on the river, but the ground was a lot softer than it looked. When I tried to back up, the trailer slid in, followed by the two passenger-side tires of my Jeep Laredo. My four-wheel-drive turned out to be useless and a rear tire started hissing steadily. Luckily, I had my AAA membership.

The first piece I read was about a bowfisherman down in Corpus Christi. Back in 2012, Brent Crawford was working on his dock when a neighbor showed up and reported a major ruckus in a shallow canal. The neighbor said the fish responsible for this splashing were as long as a car. Crawford put down his work, picked up his bow, and went to that spot with his dog. He saw a mammoth female alligator gar spawning with five smaller males between four and six feet long, so he stalked the big one. He finally took his shot and hit his mark, then saw that his unraveling nylon cord was tangled around his feet. While trying to get the line away, he wrapped it around his wrist, and the fish yanked him into the drink. Crawford's dog, however, chomped down

FIG. 30. Brent Crawford and possible Texas state record gator gar. Courtesy of Brent Crawford.

on his pant leg, and a tug of war ensued. That didn't work too well, but Crawford managed to free his hand and stand up in the canal. The fish was almost two hundred feet away, and Crawford spent the next forty-five minutes horsing it in. He finally grabbed it by its gills and shoved it up on the bank. Exhausted, Crawford sat down on the fish, took his cell phone out of its waterproof case, and called his buddy, who brought a gun. They shot the gar, tied it to a four-wheeler, and dragged it back to Crawford's place. The fish measured eight foot two and maxed out Crawford's three-hundred-pound scale. According to numerous articles, the state record for bow and arrow was 290 pounds, and the overall state record was three hundred, but that didn't matter because Crawford cleaned the fish before any wildlife agents showed up to confirm the catch.

What I most appreciate about this story is the story itself—which is of an epic battle between Man and Fish. In essence, this is why I had come to Texas and why this book exists.

The next two pieces I read concerned new protection for alligator gar by the Texas Parks and Wildlife Department (TPWD), taking effect in 2014. The new regulation makes it possible for the executive director of TPWD to suspend gator gar fishing or hunting temporarily in certain areas during spawns. What prompted this additional protection is the fact that the weather has changed, but the gar haven't. Since alligator gar spawns in Texas are becoming more complicated thanks to more dams, more drought, and less consistency in the timing of floods, TPWD biologists predict that limiting the harvest in this way will help keep the big ones around longer. Currently, successful spawns only occur every six years in Texas, and in twenty-one of the years between 1980 and 2010 reproduction was nonexistent or just plain lousy. Also, based on data collected from Choke Canyon Reservoir and the Brazos and Trinity rivers, it's estimated that about 3 percent of the state's alligator gar population is eliminated each year, and that if the annual kill rises above 5 percent, the outcome could be detrimental to sustaining future generations.

This new protection includes some stipulations on how harvested gar get reported. Though the daily limit remains one gator gar, a free tag program, much like the system used for alligators in Louisiana, is envisioned. The tag system also includes a way to report information that biologists can use to locate populations and compile useful data, like we do in Arkansas.

The next piece I read was an article entitled "How to Fish for Alligator Gar," published on the website *Wikihow.com*. This self-help article had been viewed by over 126,000 viewers, and it was full of disinformation. The first step states that alligator "gar thrive in the Mississippi river basin, from Southern Ohio and Illinois to the Gulf of Mexico": false. They certainly do not "thrive" in Ohio and Illinois. If anything, they've been stocked in Illinois and the Ohio River, but as for their status in the state of Ohio, it's not known if a single wild gator gar actually exists in the state.

Second, the piece states that gar can survive for two hours out of water, but that's all relative. Since gar have air-breathing organs similar to lungs, they can survive perhaps two days out of water, depending on the heat and humidity and other factors.

Third, the article advises using "30–100 pound test mono-filament line": also completely wrong. Whenever the word "monofilament" appears in print, it's usually because someone who doesn't understand fishing is trying to sound smart. For freshwater fishing, monofilament hardly ever exceeds thirty-pound test, and it's rarely used for gator gar. Woven or braided line is standard and can take the stress that a single strand of plastic line can't.

Fourth, the article advises that after a gar takes your bait you should "wait at least seven seconds" before setting the hook: terrible misinformation. You should wait more like five or ten minutes, depending on the size of the bait and the size of the gar. That's how long it usually takes for gar to stop running downstream, because that's when they finally take a break in weighing their take in their mouths, and that's when they swallow the bait. A few minutes after that, they'll take off again, and then it's time to set the hook.

Even worse, this article advises gilling or gaffing a big gar, which can injure it and make catch and release a moot point. Plus a gar is liable to twist when gaffed, thereby turning the gaff handle into an erratically swinging weapon that can smack someone upside the head.

The litany of bad ideas continues. "Cutting the line will leave the treble hook embedded in the fish's mouth, leaving it little chance of survival": not true at all. Basically, you want to get the hook out if you can, but sometimes proximity to teeth makes that impossible, and if that's the case, you sometimes have to let the fish go with a hook in it. But that doesn't mean it won't survive. Gar are tough, and if they swallow a hook, their digestive acids are so corrosive that they'll eventually dissolve solid steel.

I cringed as well at the last pointer, concerning cleaning alligator gar. "Nail the gar's head to a blank," the typo-riddled article states, "and work a knife from the tail up the backbone, loosening the scales. Cut the head and tail off, and then work your knife down the side of the fish. The scales should come up like a crust around the flesh underneath."

Whoever wrote this article doesn't understand gar. There ain't no knife in existence that can "loosen" gator gar scales or cut off a gar head. You have to use tin snips, or a power saw, to cut through their dentine-coated hides. Also, gar armor doesn't just peel away; it has to be worked away from the muscles and skin, a process that usually involves a knife and time. Also, there's a cartilaginous backstrap above the spine that should be removed. And if you nail a fish's head to a plank then cut it off before completely skinning it, what's the point in that?

My main objection, however, to this wiki article is that it spreads a lot of dangerous information that scientists and environmentalists have been trying to reverse for decades. By tricking amateur anglers into thinking that catching and cleaning an alligator gar is an easy fifteen-step process, this website encourages people to harm gar through ignorance.

Like the ignorance—or stupidity—that landed me up past my brake rotors in sludgy muck somewhere in Texas. And when the tow truck driver finally pulled my trailer out, followed by my Jeep, I had one punctured tire in the rear, and the other one had come off the rim. Of course, I only had one spare on board.

HOW NOT TO FISH FOR ALLIGATOR GAR:
A Wiki-Not-How by Skunked_on_the_Trinity

1. After mounting the spare, don't let the tow truck driver pump up your punctured tire, point you toward the closest town, then slap you on the back and wish you luck, such that you have to drive like a bat out of hell white-knuckling the steering wheel for seventeen miles with your flashers on because it's night and your trailer wires got munched in the mud, but the cops don't notice, and then you make it to a gas station with one pound of air left in your tire and you inflate it while asking directions to a tire shop, which you shoot for and end up driving all over town, but you make it to another gas station and pump that tire up again while again asking for directions that eventually lead you to a closed-down tire store in a run-down barrio.

2. Do not make yourself a super-stiff vodka tonic and get into your sleeping bag and recline all night long in the driver's seat while waiting for the tire guy in the morning who's in no rush to get there but comes around after your breakfast of huevos rancheros across the street and eventually gets you on the road.

3. Do not make it to the launch where you put all your gear on board and back into the rushing, roiling Trinity, where the boat refuses to come off, and then you remember that you left a padlocked cable on your engine, which is why your boat is sitting funky on your trailer and that cable is stretched out to the max, so you have to clamber out there and unlock it while people watch from an incoming boat, and it just won't unlock, but eventually it does, and then you're off.

4. Do not return to one of your favorite sandbars in the world in a river that rose ten feet in a day, because hundreds of tons of floodwaters are still rising at the rate of several inches per hour, so all you have to pull up on is a few inches of slimy mud covered in thick vegetation where two years ago you saw a six-foot rattlesnake being territorial, and because the mud's so thick that it would suck off your shoes, you have to muck around in bare feet, stepping on nettles and thistles

and sharp sticks while getting crud all over your boat, your gear, yourself, the world.

5. Do not fish at a time when the cold waters are causing all those rolling, flopping six- and seven-footers to not give a wang dang doodle about your bait, which they probably can't even see or smell because of all that extra turbulent water in the hole where gator gar are usually more concentrated, but not on that afternoon, when all you do is untangle bird's nests in your baitcasting reels while your various lines keep crossing each other because of the chaotic currents and wild eddies. Plus your most heavy-duty rod isn't casting right and there's a seven-foot yellow-bellied 150-pounder rolling just twenty yards away which you can't even reach because your line always stops three feet short of where you're trying to cast, and still that gar hangs out all day pretty much mocking you.

6. When your island goes underwater, do not move to the next best spot on the bend, which provides a place to set up a camp chair and kick back on an ever-eroding bank that's literally falling apart beneath you, but at least you've got a place to watch your lines in an area where the gar aren't—but on your lighter rod, fishing for bait with a worm, you do hook a fifteen-pound blue cat, and after five minutes of furious fighting you bring it in just in time to see your flimsy hook bend and pop out of its mouth.

7. Don't crunch around in poison ivy gathering firewood to cook a pan full of sausages and beans while the water continues to rise, and now it's too late to head back to the launch in the dark, and besides, a thunderstorm is threatening.

8. Don't stumble up to your tent, which you set up on a forty-five-degree-angled slope because that's the only place to do it, and there are no tent stakes holding it to the ground because you lost them in the mud, but still you crawl into that tent and sleeping bag with about five pounds of mucky clay stuck to your shins, then cling to your air mattress all night long, because if you don't you'll roll over and the tent will tumble into the river below, which is still rising, and your boat could float away, and damn it's cold out, because the

zipper breaks on your sleeping bag so you stay up shivering until dawn.

9. In the vapor-snaking morning, don't even try fishing again because you haven't caught anything—you're not going to catch anything, and those enormous gar don't care about your trivial bait—but at least the water has leveled out and is even starting to go down, and here comes the sun, though not one dang porpoising gar is inclined to bite.

10. On your way back to Arkansas, your feet covered with bleeding wounds, don't even try to envision all that ditch-mud on your tires coming off, because you've also picked up a layer of gravel from the boat launch so that your tires, resembling peanut-encrusted chocolate donuts, rotate for five hours straight, and your tread never sees the light of day, still buried three inches under a strange plasticky mud that hardens on the interstate but is nevertheless flexible enough to get you back to your driveway where you hose it off but can't fix your patched tire (now the spare), which will have to be replaced since the puncture is on the sidewall, which will cost you two hundred bucks, and then you have to chisel out your brake assemblies while wondering if there's any truth in the idea that what you endured was worth the effort when the obvious answer is *hell no!*

Getting my ass kicked called for drastic action. I had a job to finish. I couldn't go back and get skunked again. Hiring a guide, I figured, would be like cheating, because I'm supposed to be a gar expert. But then again, I debated with myself, you can always learn new tricks from guides, and they can take you to places you never knew existed. Hence it made sense to go back and do it right—with *guidance* from a *guide*.

So a few months later I hired Dawson Hefner and went back to gar school.

Dawson picked me up at 6:00 a.m. in the dark before the Texas dawn, and by sunup we were at the launch, which was totally covered in that slick mud I knew too well. Dawson winched his boat and trailer down the ramp and into the misting Trinity while I read a sign posted by the Texas Bowfishing Association asking bowshooters not to leave their fish at the launch, because it was "inconsiderate." This sign was a message that the culture was changing, and it impressed me a great deal.

You can usually get a feel for a guide right off the bat, and there was something I really liked about Dawson. He was young, twenty-eight years old, but highly professional. I also liked the fact that he drove a beat-up pickup truck and his sixteen-foot johnboat was nothing fancy. Having grown up in Tyler, Dawson was making a name for himself as an up and coming gator gar guide.

My goal, of course, was to get a huge one, anything over six feet long. As bait we had fresh bloody carp that Dawson had shot with a bow and arrow the night before, and he had three ten-foot cat rods on board with heavy-duty Penn spinning reels strung with 130-pound braided test. The black steel leaders started out five feet long and got a couple of inches shorter every time they had to be snipped to account for a swallowed hook. And the treble hooks surprised me because they were small—size 3.0, which is the size I usually use when fishing for catfish with chicken livers.

Dawson said they were muskie hooks, and I soon found out why they made a lot of sense. Due to their smaller size, it was a lot easier getting them unsnagged from submerged trees, compared to working with the shark-sized hooks I was accustomed to using. Plus there was less metal to corrode away, so the gars could get the hooks out of their systems faster. But best of all, there was a lot less metal for a fish to sense, so they tended to drop the bait less and swallow more frequently.

Dawson told me that mid-October was a good time of year, because the gar were fattening up for winter, so they'd eat all day. As I also discovered, the weather was ideal at this time of year, climbing only into the eighties, rather than frying you alive with temperatures topping a hundred degrees.

Dawson sped us to the spot, and then he rigged up with small chunks of carp (about a pound each), which I also found unusual. In the world

FIG. 31. Six foot ten, 135 pounds! Photo by Dawson Hefner.

of gator gar fishing, the mentality is usually "use big bait to catch big fish"—but not today.

Then it happened, in the first half hour on the river. After setting the poles up on the mud banks on holders with built-in alarms, we heard one go off. We shot over and picked up the pole and followed the float downstream. The gar stopped for a few minutes, and then it started heading upstream, right toward us. I took in the slack as the float went under the boat. Dawson told me I could hit it.

WHAM! The fish wigged out right beneath us, thumping and smacking and tossing us around. Then it shot off, towing us in circles until I eventually brought it up. The swirling surface boiled and broke, and one of the most mammoth gars I'd ever seen lurched from the depths thrashing its mega-head.

Then it dove, taking out line. I fought it, though, and brought it back, wearing it out as much as I could. I battled it for at least ten minutes, and then Dawson took a PVC pipe with a cable on it and snared it under its pectoral fins. He braced himself to haul in a fish at least a foot longer than himself, and threw his back into it. The gar resisted and fought back, but eventually came up, slid over the rail, and commenced to lash back and forth, going nuts. It even actually roared a few times.

When it finally settled down, we broke out the tape measure, and it was six foot ten! It was the biggest fish I'd ever caught in my life. It was also equal in length to the hugest gar Dawson had ever caught in his life.

We measured its girth (35.75 inches) and rigged up a harness with some rope. Attaching my heavy-duty digital scale to the PVC pipe, we each put a shoulder under it, and we lifted it as high as we could. The scale read 135 pounds.

Then came the money shot. I sat up front, Dawson wrassled it into my arms, and I posed with the fish, which neighed a few times like a horse. I also got a good look at some of the sea lice crawling on it. Those little crustaceans were the hugest I'd ever seen, a bit more sandy-colored than usual, allowing me to discern their crablike sections, which are hard to see when they're transparent like a contact lens.

The gar, however, was my main focus, but I had to let it go. I tipped it toward the water, it slid in, and I said goodbye. The slime it left on me was some of the sweetest smelling gar goo ever lacquered on me.

Coyotes howled and we got back to fishing. Dawson told me about the formula for calculating the weight of an alligator gar. You multiply the length in inches by its girth, then multiply that by its girth again, and then divide that by eight hundred and add fifteen. Dawson used the calculator function on his cell phone while I did the math on paper, and guess what? We both came up with the figure of 135 pounds, which was in agreement with my scale. Since this eliminated the need to stress the fish out any more, I put my scale away.

Less than an hour later we heard another alarm go off. We went through the same routine again, I waged another epic battle, it fought even harder than the first fish, and suddenly we had another monster gar in the boat. This one was five foot ten and 28.5 inches around, so according to the formula it weighed eighty-six pounds. This fish was also a bit stinkier than the first (I like to describe the smell of gar slime as a cross between soggy old cardboard and rotten fruit), and it had a much more assertive attitude, sometimes snapping at us.

As the morning went on, we got a runner and followed it, but it dropped the bait. Then we got a double, meaning two alarms went off at once. We grabbed both poles and got out into the current, but both fish dropped their baits, also at the same time.

We set everything back up again, and the moment the last pole was in place, all three alarms went off simultaneously. It was mayhem. Dawson grabbed one pole, I grabbed another, and we left the third on the shore. I can't remember exactly what happened, but I ended up bringing in two of those fish. My third one was five foot eight and eighty-one pounds and my fourth was six foot seven and 128 pounds!

We were now in the cherriest spot I'd ever been. It was a long muddy sandbar on a vast deep bend with clay cliffs rising on the other side. Beneath us, the chocolate murkwater was swarming with gargantu-gar.

We got two more runners with which I couldn't seal the deal, I ate a sandwich of beef jerky on wheat bread, and then it was afternoon, and the hits just kept on coming.

Especially the Big One! When I finally brought it to the surface, it was as fat around as a trashcan and pretty much the same color. It kept using its sheer weight as its main defense by diving down and sticking to the bottom. I kept horsing it up, though, and every time we saw that back breach like a submarine, neither of us could believe it.

That fish was so massive that we decided to tow it to a gravel bank, where it flopped up on shore by itself when we landed. Holy crap! This fatty measured six foot nine and thirty-eight inches in girth, which meant it was 163 pounds! It was the heaviest fish I had ever caught, and it beat Dawson's best as well.

Then we saw its tail. It had a deformed little cartoony tail, which explained why it hadn't fought so hard—because it lacked that power for flappage in the back. Its tailfin only had a quarter of the area it should have had and was probably in the process of growing back.

FIG. 32. The 163-pound mutant grotesque. Photo by Mark Spitzer.

This ancient mutant was missing six inches of tail and had once been seven foot three.

We had two more strikes after that, but one went under a log and transferred a barb to the log, and the other got off, because that's what happens sometimes. Still, there was no way I could complain. It was the best day of fishing I'd ever experienced. I caught six hundred pounds of alligator gar, of which three were six-plus-footers and two more topped five feet. Dawson told me it was the best gar trip he'd ever been on, and I was buzzing hard all the way back to the Super 8, covered in mucus and mud.

I'd been extremely impressed by how Dawson knew his stuff, and unlike some other gator gar guides I had worked with, he wasn't the least bit pretentious. He had taught himself to fish for alligator gar, and he had an incredible natural instinct for it. I learned that if a gar goes downstream then heads back up, that means you can set the hook. I also learned that if you press on a gar's gill plate, its eyeballs bulge out like a hardboiled egg. Watching Dawson watch those floats, however, I was amazed at his ability to gauge a fish's behavior underwater. He knew these fish, and he knew them well.

So I was psyched for the second day. Whereas we could have gone back to the cherry spot to catch more super-sized gar, I figured that we'd already been down that road, and I wanted to see something new. Thus we went to another spot, one I'd always wanted to explore.

Again we had a runner within the first half hour, also right under the boat. That gar gave us a good run for its size, which was somewhere in the four-foot range. But when I raised its head out of the water, the carp chunk popped out and the gar got away.

The next gar was about the same size, and I lost it in the exact same way. They kept running, and we kept after them, and each time a gar lit off, the sense of palpitation I felt was way more than it had been the day before. In short, I was thrilled to be psyched and psyched to be thrilled like I hadn't been in years—no doubt due to some personal crap I'd recently gone through, which I won't go into.

No, I take that back. I will go into it, because it does make a difference. That is, gar can make a difference when tragedy strikes. A year ago, my marriage went to hell, and I was in the worst place I'd ever been. I'd seen the worst thing a husband could see, and it took its toll on me in panic attacks and depression. I spent the next twelve months exhausting myself by traveling alone all over the West, then traveling back and forth to Minnesota by myself with constant thoughts of death and divorce eating at me like battery acid. Then, 364 days after having kicked my ex out of the house, I held my mother as she died in my arms. That was only two weeks before this fishing trip. Meaning it was about as sucky as a year can get.

But not anymore, thanks to Dawson Hefner of Texas Megafish Adventures! He got me out of that funk by connecting me with ten beautiful alligator gar, which ultimately reconnected me with what I had temporarily lost: that youthful capacity for wondering and marveling at what this world has to offer. Because like I said: gar were the cure. Or salvation. Or whatever. They gave me what I needed to get past what I needed to get past. So remember that the next time you're bumming hard. If gar can do this for me, then there's something out there that can do the same for you.

Fishing on, we caught six more good gar that day. They weren't quite as large as those of the day before, but they were still a blast to fight. The first was five foot one and 54.46 pounds, the next one four foot six and 33.5 pounds. Then I lost a six-footer that was a joy to see in the water, along with a hundred other log-sized gars I was privileged to see surface here and there. But I also caught another of five foot one and 61.7 pounds and a four-foot-sixer in the 40-pound range.

At one point we had two gars on two lines so Dawson brought in one himself while I worked on the other. Dawson's was a three-footer, and the one I had got away. So did six or seven more, but that's showbiz. I ended the day with a surprise five-foot-tenster that we thought was a turtle nosing around on the bottom. It proved to be a 71-pounder and it put up a respectable fight.

As we tied up to the shore I was in the bow, securing the line to a root, when all of a sudden a kamikaze beaver came bolting from a hole beneath the bank and leapt right under my arm and over the bow, belly-flopping into the river. I laughed and took a step back—and just in time too, because another beaver came barreling out and also leapt right over the bow, just three feet from me. Dawson was a bit freaked out by this sudden blast of beaverness. He was concerned that there might be more coming and that one might land in the boat and cause havoc.

But I was still laughing. I had just caught way more than my fair share of the coolest fish on the planet, and by gum, that's what fishing is all about. It's about landing lunkers and meeting mutants, and the escape and elation, and it's also about losing leviathans and just missing a full-on beaver attack!

Yep, it was a truly awesome fishing trip for a truly awesome fish that's right there, right now, in the south of the American West, accessible to anyone who's serious about going to Texas and getting them. There are plenty of seven-footers in that extremely successful fishery, and those fish can weigh more than three hundred pounds! They're not just run-of-the-mill grotesques, they're *our grotesques*—so why not catch and release 'em for the express selfish reason of improving our quality of life?

That's what I'm talking about.

10

Rattlesnakes at the Razorback Roundup

Working with What We've Got

Twenty hours after striking out for the Arizona-Nevada border, my yellow canoe strapped up top, I reached the summit and saw Lake Mohave below. Jagged buttes and scrubby peaks ridged both sides of a stupefying desert vista which used to contain the now impounded Colorado River. Thousand-year-old findings from Catclaw Cave and Quiburi tell us that the ancient dwellers in this faded terra-cotta terrain used to feast on a primitive fish now known as the razorback sucker—a quasi-Quasimodo with an elongated horsey head and an "inferior mouth," meaning downward-pointing sucker lips for slurping up algae and detritus.

Back in the 1980s, there used to be over sixty thousand of these bright gold suckers scouring the reservoir, but now, thanks to a damming mentality, aggressive poisoning campaigns to wipe out native fish, the introduction of over seventy non-native fish species in this river system, and extremely high selenium levels, the razorbacks have dropped to somewhere between two and three thousand adults in Lake Mohave. Still, this is an improvement over the way things used to be back in 1991 when the species was officially listed as endangered. In fact, by 2010 they were listed as "critically endangered," and by 2011 a report by Marsh &

Associates estimated that there were only thirteen wild razorbacks (as opposed to "repatriated" razorbacks) left in the reservoir.

A feral jackass shot across the dirt road and went bounding through the cacti and arrow weed as I wound down to Carp Cove for the annual Razorback Roundup. My Google searches had led me to Dr. Paul Marsh, whose Native Fish Lab is at the forefront of research for the species *Xyrauchen texanus*, meaning "razory naped fish from Texas." The geographical mistake was made by a taxonomist named Abbott back in 1860, but it sticks to this day.

Paul had been receptive to my emails and had invited me to join the effort: rounding up razorbacks with the Native Fishes Work Group, a partnership of the U.S. Fish & Wildlife Service, Bureau of Reclamation, U.S. Geological Survey, National Park Service, Nevada Department of Wildlife, Arizona Game and Fish Department, and Arizona State University. The Lower Colorado River Multi-Species Conservation Program is also involved, which includes other federal and state agencies, local tribes, independent labs, hatcheries, power companies, and conservation groups, all bent on bringing back a fish that, according to David Starr Jordan back in 1902, has "a very grotesque appearance."

"Homely looking," however, is probably a more accurate way to describe this odd-looking fish, which once ranged throughout the Colorado River Basin, from Wyoming down to Mexico and into California. Our history of constipating rivers and favoring sport fish has reduced the razorback range to an estimated tenth of what it once was. This remnant population, though, is the largest, healthiest, most genetically diverse population left, and Marsh & Associates are committed to bringing these fish back up to snuff—if that's even possible. As a leading researcher on razorback suckers, Paul has been waging his crusade for more than thirty years, so I was glad to take part and learn as much as I could about this bizarre casualty of our culture, which has always been quick to extirpate native fish in favor of myopic sport fisheries and tourism industries fueled by short-term gain.

If this sounds like I'm biased, it's because I am. In my mind, valuing jet skis and pontoon party barges, plus trophy bass from the other half of the continent at the expense of what God intended to exist in this dramatically rich geography is just plain blasphemy. And I say this with all sincerity, even if I consider myself an atheist.

Paul couldn't make it due to a family emergency, but his crew was on the scene: Jamie Wisenall, Chase Ehlo, Kristen Humphrey, Aaron Burgad, and Brittany Woodward, led by Senior Project Manager Brian Kesner. They were a foxy young bunch of aquatic biologists and fishery assistants dressed in ironic t-shirts sporting words like "SPORK" and "GONE SQUATCHIN'," so they had a sense of humor. They received me warmly and within the hour we were on the water, checking PIT tag scanners for signs of razorback action and setting three-hundred-foot trammel nets.

Within another hour we were sitting around the campfire eating spaghetti and drinking from a five-gallon keg of Brian's homebrewed "Cheap-Ass Ale," all of us passionate in our conviction that the razorback sucker has just as much right to be here as we do, right now, reclaiming our natural heritage. Because if we don't try, we suck in a way much worse than the humpback sucker—which is another name for razorbacks but not to be confused with humpback or razorback chubs (*Gila cypha*), a species also redlisted as "threatened" in this system.

We went out that night with high-powered lights and minnow traps, and we cut across to the Nevada side under the black-as-hell sky pin-pricked by all the stars of infinity, then motored to Tequila Cove, which was buzzing with Bureau of Reclamation and National Park Service activity. There were boats all over the place, nets spread with blinking floats, divers placing scanners underwater, and buckets full of razorback larvae, which my hosts pointed out in the lake. They were swimming just beneath the surface, barely a centimeter long and spermy shaped, squiggling to survive.

FIG. 33. Brittany Woodward with razorback sucker. Photo by Mark Spitzer.

That was why Chase—our hardy, jolly camp cook—had brought along the minnow traps baited with fish pellets. The idea was to catch sunfish in order to test the DNA of their stomach contents; their digestive acids, along with those of other non-native predators, are pretty much responsible for destroying most of every razorback spawn in these waters. Hence, every year at this time, the Native Fish Working Group collects fifteen to twenty-five thousand larval razorbacks and transports them to the Willow Beach National Fish Hatchery, where they're raised to over a foot long, then released to "repatriate" the system. But when nineteen-inch razorbacks are found in the guts of transplanted striped bass, the process can only be frustrating and slow going for those aiming to remedy what we screwed up when we decided to play God by reconfiguring the natural order of things.

But there I go again, bringing in religion, when the point is that we set those minnow traps then shot off to check the nets, which were six feet deep with 1.5-inch white mesh. Basically, we'd pull up to the first float, and then the crew would line up along the starboard side and work their way down the net, lifting and untwisting, while I knelt on the deck staring at what our spotlight lit up—which included crazy amounts of obese carp and football-sized smallmouth bass tangled in a jumbo mess. But there were catfish as well, plus yellow bullheads, gizzard shad, and an occasional softshell turtle or largemouth—all of these, from our point of view, "invasive species."

In the third net we pulled up a nice three-pound razorback, just over twenty inches long (we recorded the lengths in millimeters, but I'm converting to inches). It was a glittering, golden female twisted up like no tomorrow, but our crew of professionals knew how to untangle it swiftly and get it into an onboard tub.

The razorback was scanned for tags, and fin clips were taken and preserved in alcohol. If a fish lacked a tag, one was injected into the abdomen. That was the process and protocol, and in the end the fish were released. The data gets plugged into the grand equation, and then we have a better estimate of how many razorbacks there are in the reservoir. Brian deemed this particular fish a "fresh releaser," meaning it had recently been caught and accounted for.

Not long after that we caught an even larger humpback, this one just over twenty-two inches, with an even more prominent hunchback keeling up from its shoulders. We got it into the tub, where I saw it leap up and shudder like a dynamo, refusing to accept its confinement. It even tail-danced on the surface of that tub, driving forth, shooting to shoot out. This image burned itself into my brainpan, that humpy profile driving and striving to continue existing.

Most of the razorback spawning in this system had occurred the week before, so most of these fish were spent of milt or roe. One of our fish was ripe and bulging with eggs, so was easily identified as a female. The experts I was running with, however, could tell what gender the fish were by a glance at the cloaca or tuberculated tail (meaning having bumps, on males).

I slept in my bedroll in the Jeep and we struck out at eight in the morning. The sun was a lot brighter than the day before, and it allowed me to see the rubbled bottom clearly thirty or forty feet beneath the hull. It was as barren as the moon and coated with algae, and when a fish swam by you could see the details down to the scales.

We began pulling in loads of sparkling four-pound bass, plus great bulging carp and plenty of channel cats. The third net held a bright, coppery three-pound razorback, and then we got the largest, most robust humpback we'd meet on this trip. It was 26.5 inches long (they don't get much longer than a yard) and probably seven pounds.

After that, we caught a twenty-three-incher missing a pectoral fin, followed by a twenty-incher. I picked up the latter to take a picture of the butterfly-flare of its nubby textured lips, and that was when it jettisoned a pale yellow string of eggs. Since I had my camera in hand, I hit "record" on the video function and taped the show, the crew laughing in the background, amused by the spewing roe. To see this video, go to YouTube and type in "rattlesnakes and razorbacks."

So far all the suckers we'd caught were female, but then we got our first male—and an old-school male at that, measuring just over two feet long. It was one of the biggest males most of the crew had ever seen. As in many fish species, the female razorbacks grow larger than the males.

We then sped away from the nets and released our humpacks back to the current—which is nothing compared to the flow they were designed for. The Colorado River used to have a much more turbid system, where their specialized backs provided for stability in much murkier waters.

Upstream there were more razorbacks in the river, as well as in Lake

Mead above that and Lake Havasu below. It was good to know that even if razorbacks have been extirpated from most of their native range, other states have similar reclamation projects in the works.

Why? Because it's the law. When a species is listed as endangered, we can't just stand by and watch its decline; we're required to take remedial action. Nevertheless, chatroom chatter among avid anglers includes complaints about millions of dollars being spent on fish that some regard as worthless suckers, so there's a lot of criticism leveled at conservation biologists, who sometimes seem as if they're spinning their wheels trying to bring the humpback numbers up.

This is just one aspect of the politics plaguing razorbacks. We'll get to some others in a bit.

That afternoon, rather than accompany a crew of divers placing scanners underwater to collect data on tagged razorbacks passing by, I elected to go fishing instead. After all, I'd brought my canoe along, and I'd also purchased a fishing license and an invasive species decal—even though the definition of "invasive" seems to be a matter of opinion around here, depending on where your allegiances lie.

With the sun high in the sky and blazing straight down, I paddled out into the cove, where I found myself standing up in the middle to get a better view, paddling as if on a paddleboard. In the greenish-tinted crystalline water, I could clearly see the bass below, some of them nesting in graveled beds, others just wandering wherever they pleased.

I had a silver #4 Mepps spinner on my line with which I stalked my quarry, taking a paddle then taking a cast across the glassy surface of the lake. I found I could locate a fish and target it, but because they could see me as well, they were easily spooked. In spite of that disadvantage, I finally got a follow from one, and it was a pleasure to witness it hit right before my eyes. I then led it into my net and landed it, a beautiful green-gold smallie, about the size of a size-15 shoe.

We'd been hauling in these fish en masse, but this one was different.

For one thing, I caught it on rod and reel, and for another, I caught it by myself. And that was when it hit me: there's a unique tension in this neck of the woods, where a battle rages between biologists and fisherman, and I occupy a space between them. Like millions of others in this world, I seek the thrill of horsing in a leaping lunker—but I also want to see native species take back their turf

As I continued working the shoreline, I came upon a retired guy hanging out in a lawn chair on the shore, his RV parked behind him. An hour before he'd been illegally chainsawing mesquite trees for firewood, and the day before he'd been watching us with binoculars as we hauled in the trammel nets.

"What are you guys fishing for with those nets?" he called to me.

"Razorback suckers," I replied.

"Why?" he asked. "Are they endangered?"

"Yep," I replied, and took another cast.

Then he asked a flummoxing question: "Can you eat 'em?"

That was when another smallmouth hit, so I gave it my full attention and brought it in. By the time I got the hook out of its mouth and strung it up, the largest smallmouth I'd ever caught, I'd drifted too far to continue the conversation.

Back at camp, I told Jamie what that guy had said, and she said, "Yeah, I have that conversation all the time. I don't understand why they always ask that."

"Maybe it's because they're looking for a utility for razorbacks," someone else put in. "As if they should be kept around only because they serve a purpose."

But do they serve a purpose? I'm still scratching my head on this.

Rob Clarkson from the Bureau of Reclamation in Glendale and geneticist Tom Dowling from Wayne State University arrived that afternoon with news that a shocking boat would be coming along shortly to zap sunfish for stomach content analysis. Meanwhile, Jamie and Brian sat

FIG. 34. Mohave rattlesnake. Photo by Mark Spitzer.

down in the shade to record data on the razorbacks we'd caught. Brian had a laptop with information corresponding to tag numbers, and Jamie was jotting notes into a logbook.

It turned out that the fish with the missing pectoral fin had been released in 2009, and the "fresh releaser" from the night before was a four-year-old razorback once tagged by Marsh & Associates. Also, the bigger female from the night before had been released in 1999, so that meant it was probably eighteen or nineteen years old—which wasn't a spectacular growth rate, but at least it was still in the system. The biggest female of the bunch, on the other hand, was found to have been released in 2005, so it was twelve or thirteen years old, depending on its age at the time of its liberation from the Vats of Man. The most interesting news, though, was in regard to the big old male, which we found out had been released in 1996, making it over twenty years old.

Wild specimens have been found to reach ages of fifty years, but due
to predation, the repatriates in this system would be lucky to get as old
as this male.

Since there was a lot of down time in the afternoons, it didn't take long
for a bunch of us to congregate on the shore, where we drank some of
Brian's Cheap-Ass Ale. Jamie got up to get some Cheezits and was gone
for a bit. Then we heard a cry from the brush.

We went running over, and there was a five-foot-long Mojave rattlesnake all coiled up, shaking that rattle like a maraca. Its black tongue was
flickering in and out, and it was sending the message to stay back. Still,
I got within four feet, took some pictures, and then shot some video. It
had crossed the path in front of Jamie, and she had almost stepped on it.

I then headed up the trail to see if I could get a cell phone signal,
since my plan was to stop at my father's house in New Mexico on my
way back and take him the bass I'd caught. Along the trail I decided
to check out a recently vacated camping spot on the water, and guess
what I found? Another rattler. This one was only three and a half feet
long, but since it was on the move I got a better look at its tail, which
had a few inches of black and white stripes right beneath the rattle. I
shot some video of this one too. Like the bass and carp and catfish we
had caught in pursuit of razorback suckers, I considered these snakes
a "bycatch" as well.

That night we went out to sample larvae at a backwater known as AJ
(short for "Arizona Juvenile"). It was dark when we got to the gravel
beach, which was populated by large yellow leathery toads that hardly
flinched when we picked them up.

We went over the berm of a mini-reservoir, where the team immediately began setting up lights in the water. The spawn were attracted

to these lights, and we scooped them up with dip nets and put them in a bucket. Then we put them in vials of alcohol to test their DNA later.

Tonight we were experimenting with Everclear, which was cheaper than the big jugs of lab-grade, 190-proof, non-denatured ethanol. According to Tom Dowling, Everclear had worked well in Michigan. There was also an interest in trying out vodka and gin—but not the vodka back at camp, which was reserved for us after the daily work was done.

It didn't take long for the larvae to show up, swarming the lights like gangbusters. I caught the first one but put down my net when one of those toads came swimming my way. I held out my hand, and it swam right into my palm and didn't seem to mind when I picked it up and took some photographs. He was a gentle fellow, chirping away agreeably, so I let him go.

With our vials full, we then shot out to check the nets, and I spoke to Tom about the purpose of the samples we had taken. He explained that they were working to establish more of these isolated backwaters, which work well to raise spawn. Basically, they take a hundred adult males and a hundred adult females and put them in a pond, then let nature take its course. The samples we took would be tested for genetic variation to predict reproductive success.

I asked if these areas were predator-free, and Tom said they were—fishwise, that is. Once, though, they put two hundred adults in one of these pools, and when they returned later that year, the fish were all gone. Tom suspected cormorants, so there were still some kinks to work out.

In essence, the conservation biologists focusing on razorback suckers felt that the backwater systems they were now concentrating on were better suited than the hatchery for razorback recruitment, but of course there'd been major investments in the latter. So the question, when different parties were warring over resources, was which method to use to reach their objective.

Anyhow, we got two more razorbacks in the net, then motored back to camp to test the efficacy of the vodka—but not for purposes of testing DNA.

The next morning I played hooky again. I wanted to try a huge Mepps #5 spinner with two flashy rotating blades. It was constructed like a cowgirl lure for muskie, and it was chromy and red, and because bass hate red, I knew they'd go for that spinner. It takes a certain snap of the rod tip to get the action to kick in, and then you get a highly tangible vibing in your line that you can always feel thrumming through the water.

Within ten minutes, I caught a little guy, not much bigger than the lure itself. It took some manipulating to get the treble hook out of its mouth, but my theory held true that you don't need a pliers to unhook a fish. All you need is patience for backing the barb from whence it came. I let that bass go.

It was way more overcast than the day before, which accounted for why the bite was less. Also, because I couldn't see the fish as well, I couldn't target them as much. It was good to be out there in a t-shirt and shorts with the wind on my skin after being holed up for weeks by snow and ice in Arkansas. So as I cast, I reflected on bass, which have become the norm for recreational angling across the country. In this lake the smallmouth are dominant, but there are also plenty of stripers out there, wolfing down razorbacks.

Two months before, Hippy and I had gone out on Lake Norfork in Arkansas, which is also a giant reservoir, where we took on the subfreezing windchill. Like many lakes across the country, this system has been stocked with stripers. They're primarily a saltwater fish, but they've taken so well to fresh water that this doesn't matter. They grow fast and big and they're ferocious predators.

With instruction from our guide James Nichols, we had managed to land a number of whopper stripers. I wondered at the time if stripers were grotesque enough to qualify for this book. But by the end of that freezing day, staring at those streamlined, perfect-looking fish stacked up in the live well—they just looked too flawless and pretty to be lumped among underdogs.

Stripers lack that freaky factor that razorbacks have in spades. Or, to put it another way, humpbacks are like the unappreciated, weird-looking Jan Brady-fish of American waters compared to the much more glamorous Marcia Brady-bass of an engineered continent. We might say that our mainstream aesthetics of beauty for women are mirrored in the dynamics of our communal vision of which fish have value and which don't. Bass embody what our culture desires in fish, even though the consequences of valuing this model are highly destructive.

It's hard for a strange-looking sucker with inferior lips to compete for our hearts against the sexy allure of bass. In a sense, that's what this whole book is about: trying to re-envision how we look at fish we label "grotesque" so that we don't keep making the same mistakes. When settlers in the American West, for example, decided that gar were expendable because of their demonic appearance, generations of mass extermination ensued. This biased attitude encouraged faulty science, which led to a proliferation of misinformation that we are still trying to correct. The result was an overall weakening of our freshwater fisheries along with the fact that our preconceptions regarding gar stigmatized a valuable food source that other cultures are wise to exploit.

In the meantime, the gang returned to Carp Cove having caught only one razorback, the smallest of the expedition. It was less than a foot long, a spritely little golden cutie. But as they pulled in the last net in the bay, there were two more tangled in the mesh, plus a baby striper, no doubt full of razorback spawn.

The annual meeting of the tribes was set for that afternoon. Every year the razorback sucker hunters and gatherers of the Native Fish Working Group meet at the Marsh & Associates base camp for lunch, then pow-wow about everyone's progress and where they're at. This year, Chase presided over a grill full of hot dogs, hamburgers, turkey burgers, and some veggie fare for the less carnivorous.

Before the meeting started I interviewed a fishery expert from the

Bureau of Reclamation who I'd been told was very opinionated and would give me some colorful commentary. I was trying to get a perspective on the politics, and he was glad to talk. I knew there was a tension between fishermen and biologists, and I'd also been informed that what the biologists want and what the fishery engineers build doesn't always work out for what both groups intend. One razorbackologist had told me that when government gets involved things move slowly, and that those who know are often ignored; he also said that when states get involved, they've got their own priorities, which depend upon the politicians in power. And then there are the sportfishermen, who don't want to see their favorite fishing hole turned into a native fish sanctuary.

The Bureau of Reclamation biologist went into detail about the cold water problems with the Willow Beach Hatchery, which is responsible for raising most of the razorbacks released back into this system. He told me how the hatchery had initially used water from below the dam, but when the temperature of that water became inconsistent they began digging wells, which provide warmer water: good for razorbacks but not so good for the invasive quagga mussel. The razorback community was shooting for a quagga-free facility, but a lawsuit was brought against the hatchery for not supporting trout as much, because trout require colder quagga-free water. Constituents complained, and Senator John McCain got involved, demanding more attention to non-native fish. "Sometimes one angry fisherman has more clout than a roomful of conservation biologists," the Bureau agent told me.

The meeting was beginning, so we settled into a circle of fold-out chairs and coolers for benches. There were thirty to forty people present. The Bureau of Reclamation had accounted for nineteen humpbacks, the National Park Service had netted twenty-six, the U.S. Fish & Wildlife Service brought in thirty-three, and Arizona Game and Fish and Marsh & Associates each had nine. The Multi-Species Conservation Program was also there, as was the Nevada Department of Wildlife.

Brian emceed and soon gave the floor to Ty Wolters from Reclamation, who announced that over fifteen thousand razorbacks had been stocked into the system that year, which we knew wouldn't last long—because that's what happens every year with this highly complex operation, Still, it look as though the little steps are gradually adding up. As Brian told me earlier, he thinks we're a generation away from changing public attitudes, which will be key to this project's success.

We learned that nineteen razorbacks had been fitted with sonic tags so that their movements could be tracked. The resulting data showed that razorbacks stocked near Willow Beach were staying where they were, but seven fish from the lower end of the lake had moved upstream. There were submersible underwater receivers, or SURs, scattered throughout the lake, capturing data as we spoke.

Another interesting topic of conversation was that larvae gathered from Yuma Cove were dying when placed in buckets of water that came right out of the lake where those larvae had been harvested. So far, there had been two hundred razorback casualties, and no one could figure it out.

Trish Delrose from the Bureau of Reclamation then told us that we were on track to collect the year's objective of seventeen thousand larvae. Thirteen thousand had already been taken from Tequila Cove, 764 from Kayak Cove, and a handful from other spots. There were still a couple of days left, and then these seventeen thousand would be raised in various facilities.

A question came up as to whether the mark-recap population estimates from the nets were "representative" of the scanning data being collected from the PIT scanners out in the lake. The answer was that the number of fish contacted by both methods was comparable so far.

Another topic was to release bigger razorbacks in the lake to ensure better survival rates. The figure of forty centimeters (just over sixteen inches) was suggested. This figure was met with general agreement. Paul Marsh told me later that fifty centimeters (nearly twenty inches) was preferable, but he added: "In reality, the size is what the hatchery gives you."

Rob Clarkson then raised the question of the day: "How is this program going in regard to meeting its goal of fifty thousand?" Apparently this number had been established as a goal back in the 1980s, but at this point there were less than three thousand adults in the lake.

An old-timer with suspenders responded to that, and some others responded to him. What I gathered from this discussion was that things had changed, and that the overall number wasn't as important as the diversity of the genetic broodstock. Back when the goal of fifty thousand was established, the lake was full of trout. Now, however, the trout had been replaced by bass, including the dreaded striper, the razorback's second worst nightmare after ourselves.

Tom Dowling was the go-to man on this subject, and he proclaimed that we want to maintain five thousand adult razorbacks for genetic diversity, with an ultimate goal of ten to twenty thousand scattered across all backwaters. He added that it would be good for this group to interact more with the Lake Mead and Lake Havasu groups, to which someone replied that this was already happening. Tom ended the discussion by simply stating, "We have what we have to work with."

After the meeting adjourned, I packed up my canvas chairs and began my goodbyes to some of the best damn company I'd ever hung out with. Kristen asked if I'd gotten enough information.

"Too much," I told her as I got into my Jeep. I felt that in investigating this fish I'd turned up a lot more questions than I knew what to do with, information I couldn't even consider considering. The main question seemed to be: What can this species offer us beyond biodiversity?

For other marginalized fish, there are often utilities that apply, such as managing roughfish populations or possibilities as food sources or for medicine. But with the razorback sucker, the question of why it should be preserved at such a high cost continues to cause divisions. According to a 2010 article in *High Country News*, "In the Lower Basin, the [razorback] is part of a federal conservation plan, a $626 million, 50-year, 43-species effort launched in 2005. In the Upper Basin, more than $120 million in federal funds has already been spent on razorback sucker recovery efforts. According to some estimates, an additional $84 million could be spent by 2023."

I'd been thinking about this question of utility. I hadn't arrived at a full answer, but I had at least satisfied myself with a partial answer as to what razorback suckers are good for. According to *Animal Diversity Web*, humpback suckers "are detritivorous and help perform the critical job of biodegradation. In addition to eating insects, crustaceans, and algae, razorbacks consume detritus and break it down so that it can be recycled back through the system." Hence, if fishermen like the clarity of these reservoirs and value seeing fish in order to target them, then it would be to our advantage to encourage this recovery program, because suckers are good for keeping bodies of water clean. Also, now that there's less of a current in what was formerly a more active riparian system, tons of algae in Lake Mohave risk growing out of control. Algae, of course, affect nitrate levels, so at some point anglers might find themselves dealing with oxygen issues in these waters. It's therefore advisable to pump up the numbers of razorbacks to ensure the future of sport fish in the system.

Ultimately though, more than utility is involved. If we don't try to get razorback numbers up to a sustainable level, the consequences are unconscionable, and it's a question of character. As Dr. Chuck Minckley stated in the *Endangered Species Bulletin*, "What we do is fundamentally no different than propagating the California condor. . . . When things get too rough in the wild because of man's actions, man has the responsibility to step in and take corrective actions. If we didn't, razorbacks would go extinct." But there's something even beyond this: if we let such a strange, intriguing, good-natured creature get flushed away in favor of more glorified fish, then we're throwing away a distinctive native species that is actually part of ourselves—our history, our heritage, the whole damn enchilada. Because if we allow razorbacks to disappear, that's an action that is literally part genocide, definitely part suicide, unquestionably ecocide, and an overall abomination (a word that literally means "away from man").

The experts I'd been working with for several days all knew this, but the problem, of course, is illuminating the unenlightened. And that's what we've got to work with—plus doing even more of what we're doing, which is fixing what we messed up.

So with that, I took one last look at Lake Mohave, mumbled an almost inaudible "amen," and set my sights on the hills ahead, everything coated in a layer of fine desert dust.

11

All Hail the Pikeminnow Bounty

Applying *Anamnesis* in the Northwest
as a Working Model for Fisheries

Centuries ago, a six-foot-long, one-hundred-pound, semi-carpy rough-fish known as the white salmon of the Colorado River used to range from Wyoming to the desert Southwest, through the same turf (or lack thereof) as the razorback sucker. This wide-mouthed giant, once an important food source for Native Americans, was basically wiped out by the settlers, whose drainage systems and dams threw an extra-large monkey wrench into this species' long-distance spawning migrations. The Colorado squawfish (also known as whitefish, white salmon, or salmon) is also the largest member of the minnow family in North America. But since the name squawfish isn't exactly politically correct, the American Fisheries Society changed its name to pikeminnow for the same reason that jewfish evolved into goliath grouper.

Like a few other grotesques in the Colorado Basin system, the Colorado pikeminnow was eventually listed as an endangered species. State fisheries have been trying to rebuild populations.

A pikeminnow cousin, however, exists in the Pacific Northwest, and its conservation status in Washington, Oregon, and Idaho is the exact opposite of the Colorado pikeminnow's. The northern pikeminnow

FIG. 35. Biologist holding colorado pikeminnow. Courtesy of *World Records Freshwater Fishing*, www.fishing-worldrecords.com.

(formerly northern squawfish, or Columbia River dace, or Columbia pikeminnow) doesn't grow much longer than two and a half feet, but its reputation has surpassed such lengths due to its voracious predation on a much more coveted fish. Scott Foster, author of *Pikeminnow Rewards*, sums up the situation well:

> Their primary diet, thanks to the dams on the Columbia River drainage, is juvenile salmon. . . . Dams bring fish migration to a standstill. When juvenile salmon encounter a dam, they gather and circle, apparently not knowing what to do about the cement obstruction. Many are pulled into the electric generating turbines, along with millions of gallons of water. They drop through a water channel that focuses the flowing water on the big turbine propellers, and if they survive the fall down the water channel and the spin around the turbine, the young salmon then shoot out the bottom of the dam, often into the

mouths of waiting predators. Obviously, screens need to be in place, and they are, but the screens can't catch them all, so even a weak swimmer like the pikeminnow has a good chance at an easy meal by simply waiting downriver of a dam for the disoriented salmon to tumble past.

Thus the northern pikeminnow has become a pestilence for a multi-million-dollar salmon-based tourism and commercial fishing industry, which has also taken a huge hit from dams and development, not to mention the stream-destroying practices of the timber business. The pikeminnow, though, gets the brunt of the blame, to the point that a bounty has been placed on its grotesquely big-lipped head.

The Bonneville Power Administration began funding the Pikeminnow Sport-Reward Program in 1991 in an effort to rid the Columbia and Snake rivers of as many of these fish as possible. Anglers are now paid five dollars each for their first twenty-five pikeminnows, six bucks a piece for twenty-six to two hundred, and eight dollars per fish beyond that mark. The top pikeminnow assassin, Nikolay N. Zaremskiy, caught 9,532 in 2010, which earned him over $81,000 in squawfish-squashing income that year for five months of work. Zaremskiy continues to net such figures, and there are other bounty hunters not too far behind him, who regularly turn in fish at pikeminnow stations throughout the Columbia River Gorge.

So I went out to Washington State to investigate this ambitious program, embedding myself as a war correspondent of sorts in this battle raging in the Northwest.

The free Pikeminnow Fishing Clinic was held at the Sportsman's Warehouse in Kinnewick, and about sixty anglers were in attendance. Most were retired men, but there were some tattooed women and awkward teens present, not to mention a handful of *Duck Dynasty*–looking biker dudes sporting camo-colored sleeveless shirts. We were squished between the reels and the men's clothing, forty chairs occupied and standing room only for the rest of the attendees. Literature was distributed and the workshop kicked in.

John Hone from the Washington Department of Fish and Wildlife started off by informing everyone that northern pikeminnows are not "suckerfish," as they're commonly called. He then mentioned that since they are native species, the goal is not to exterminate them but to control their mushrooming numbers. I'd just read on pikeminnow.org that the objective of the program is "to reduce the average size and curtail the number of larger older fish," and that "Results indicate the program is successful. . . . Predation on juvenile salmonids has been cut by an estimated 40%."

As an incentive to the regular bounty the program also offers a $500 reward for catching pikeminnows with blue spaghetti tags beneath their dorsal fins. If you catch one of these, you're advised not to remove the tag. Of course, all anglers must be licensed and must turn in their own fish to the station where they registered prior to fishing.

Hone explained that Mormon crickets are the best live bait for pike-minnow, but chicken livers also work. Night crawlers were mentioned, and that got me thinking about Samuel L. Calvin's how-to book *Catch Northern Pikeminnow*, in which he recommends "cut bait (strips cut from fish), fish entrails, skin from fried chicken, salmon eggs, grasshoppers, crayfish tails, and shrimp."

Things were then turned over to Tim Histand, a retired construction worker who is now a full-time pikeminnow angler. According to the *Seattle Times*, Histand earned over $20,000 in 2012 for catching 2,702 northern pikeminnows. Basically, his talk was on what type of gear to use and how to do it.

Histand showed us an eight-foot, medium-action rod with a standard baitcasting reel. It was rigged with a twenty-inch, ten-pound fluoro-carbon leader on ten-pound braid. He had two #4 hooks on a rubber lamprey lure and a half-ounce cannonball drop weight on six inches of line leading up to a tri-eyed swivel. Like a Caribbean rig, the idea was that the weight sits on the bottom and the fish takes out line until the hook is set ("but don't pop 'em too hard," Histand advised). Histand also recommended a "plunking" action (lifting the weight a few inches off the bottom every once in a while), and he said the best lure was either a rubber tube or a grub.

Histand then discussed where to fish (in the current, near structure, on humps or rock piles, "but they can be anywhere") and the best time of day to fish (evenings or early mornings, "but some people fish at night"). He noted that hot weather is good, because when more people use electricity, more water gets released from the dams, so there's more current, and the fish get more aggressive.

Someone asked if he ever uses a net, and Histand replied that he just plops them into the boat, because that's the method he prefers. He also said that he prefers lures over live bait, though those who catch the most pikeminnows tend to rely on live bait.

For a lot of the questions from the crowd, Histand's answers seemed to be based on what works for an individual. For instance, when somebody asked how often one should fish (which I thought was a pretty strange question), Histand replied that it depends on what you want to do. For example, if you're just out to have a good time with your kids, go out on the weekends; but if you want to earn big money, then get out there as much as you can.

Histand said that when pikeminnow hit, they hit hard. But as a rule, when you get them in the boat, they tend to go completely still. Plus you get a lot of bycatch in the Columbia River system, including species like smallmouth bass, walleye, and catfish. Histand didn't mention sturgeon, but from reading Foster's book I knew they were probable too, as were peamouths, which are often confused with pikeminnows but can be distinguished by their rounded (not flattened) head and the fact that the mouth ends before the eye.

Someone then asked how many fish Histand catches on an average day, and he responded that he couldn't answer that because every day has different conditions. The questioner kept pressing. Histand said he'd caught thirty-eight the day before. The questioner then responded "See," as if he'd proved that calculating an average catch was indeed possible.

We were now well into a question and answer session, and I found myself starting to drift off because a lot of the questions involved topics already discussed. Many in the crowd seemed concerned with how to earn a living wage, and a lot of the answers were to go with what works best for you.

One of the more interesting questions was what to do with a fish under nine inches long. Do you throw it back to eat more salmon smolt, or do you eradicate it? Or do you throw it back to become bigger so someone else can catch it later and make at least five bucks?

"Well," Histand replied, "I put them back in the river." He then explained that those little ones probably won't make it anyway. I suspect his underlying message was that being handled by humans doesn't increase survival rates.

"Have they spawned yet?" someone asked. It was almost mid-June, and Hone replied yes, and that the spawn had happened "three weeks early, at least." He added that northern pikeminnow spawn at fifty-eight degrees, and it was currently sixty-four on the Snake.

Seeing that things were winding down, and since I wanted to get a tackle specialist to help me find the gear I needed before the other anglers started going for the same, I slunk back into the crowd and made my way toward the equipment. One-hundred-and-fifty bucks later, I left the store with a brand new reel, a bag full of tackle, and an out-of-state fishing license. I was more than ready to hit the river.

But first I had to visit a dam fisherman.

Eric Winther, project leader for the Columbia River Predator Control Program of the Washington Department of Fish and Wildlife, had connected me with Scott Mengis, lead pikeminnow fisherman for the Dalles and John Day dams. The crew of four professional anglers worked full-time fishing these sites to remove pikeminnows from the river. This was an aspect of the program I had to know more about.

I met Scott at the pikeminnow station at the Dalles on the Oregon side of the river, and we went over to the park and sat down at a picnic table. Having just fished all day in the freakishly intense sun, he was looking for some shade.

Scott had worked this job for six years, two as fisherman-in-chief. It was a demanding job that required him to show up at 4:00 a.m. four days a week and fish ten hours per day, rain or shine. And sometimes when it shines, and especially in August, the concrete can heat up to 120 degrees.

"We catch them on rod and reel with tubes," Scott explained, "then scan them for PIT tags and measure them. We record data like weight and time of day, then put them in coolers and process them out of the system—even the small ones."

Scott had some figures with him. In 2010 the dam-site fishermen removed 962 pikeminnows from the Columbia. In 2011 they took only 204; but for some reason that was a limited six-week period. In 2012 the numbers rose to 1,065, and in 2013 the total was 1,515. The year 2014 saw 2,700 pikeminnows removed through this method, and the 2015 figures so far were up to 4,263.

I did some calculating in my head. In 2014 just over 164,000 pikeminnows had been eliminated by bounty hunters. This meant that dam-site anglers caught nearly 2 percent of what sport-reward anglers had taken out. So if the total number of fish removed by pikeminnow anglers in 2014 was consistent for this year, with dam-fishermen on track to doubling their numbers in 2015, we'll see about 4 percent of the total catch removed through this method this year, if not more. This means that dam-site fishing is getting more and more effective, and it might not be too long before the figures rise to 5 percent, 6 percent, and over time, perhaps we can meet the 50 percent target goal.

But the other thing is this: the dam-site anglers don't just take out a small but significant chunk of the pikeminnow catch; they also collect data in the process—and not just on pikeminnows. Data are collected for catfish, walleye, sturgeon, bass, peamouth, sculpin, and other species. These bycatches, though, are released to swim another day, but probably not the three burbot that were recently caught, because of their potential to take over systems like the Flaming Gorge Reservoir in Wyoming and

Utah. Burbot, however, are native to the Columbia, and if only three are caught for every four thousand pikeminnows captured, that means they're not a very big a threat in this system at the moment. But who knows? Those numbers could change.

"There are lots of weird currents," Scott went on, "and we fish right on the bottom. It takes a long time to learn how to hunt them." He added that the turbines really stir up the flow and help to oxygenate the water, which, in turn, riles up the pikeminnows.

I asked Scott about the biggest pikeminnow he'd ever seen. His answer was six hundred millimeters, or 23.58 inches. He added that they'd recently caught a six-pound-eleven-ouncer. The International Game Fish Association lists the current world record at seven pounds, fourteen ounces. Still, a weight of 13.5 pounds is recorded on sites like the *Encyclopedia of Life*, which echo information from *Wikipedia*. The website *Fishing World Records* cites a figure of twenty-eight pounds, eleven ounces, but they categorize northern pikeminnows as "carps over 10 kg," when technically that ain't the case.

Circling back to his team, Scott said that two members fished a dam at a time. Whereas Scott worked for the state, his crew was employed by the Pacific States Marine Fishery Commission.

I asked Scott what improvements he'd seen in the last few years for the salmon fishery specifically. After all, that's what the pikeminnow program was all about.

"In general," he replied, "it seems like we're finding a record number of smolt at the John Day Dam and that pikeminnow sizes are getting smaller." The implication was that the pikeminnow program is paying off.

After that we went back to Scott's truck, and he showed me his gear. The rods were about nine feet long and equipped with 5000-size bait-casting reels strung up with twenty-pound woven line. The leaders were fifteen-pound PowerPro and the drop weights were different sizes. He also had some ounce-plus egg weights used for fishing from the bank. As for lures, Scott showed me a 2.5-inch smoke-colored tube with copper flakes and white fringe and told me that this was "the most productive" lure.

That being all I needed to know, I thanked him and took off.

"We need to get you rigged up properly," Scott Foster told me, sitting across the picnic table with his shaggy white sideburns and calming demeanor. "What you've got just isn't professional."

We were at the Eagle Creek campsite on the Columbia River, and he should know what a proper pikeminnow rig looks like, since he wrote the book on catching this fish. I'd tracked Scott down online and now we were drinking beers, our pasts converging: Scott with his pseudonym and MFA in creative writing and studies in art history, which later evolved into a career in insurance, from which he had now retired, and me with what you know so far.

Scott took out two tiny circle-type hooks and a regular old swivel. I had thrown my pole in his boat a half hour before, and he'd seen my jimmy-rigged pole. Basically, I had tried to copy his setup, but having a limited supply of tackle, I had improvised by using three 3/8-ounce weights to substitute for a one-ounce egg weight, and my single hook was way too big.

"You go five times around the shaft like this," Scott demonstrated, wrapping monofilament around the hook about eight inches from the end of the line. Then, securing the hook to the line, he tied the other hook four fingers beneath the first one and clipped off the excess line. Scott cut the other end of the line about three feet above the top hook, tied on the swivel, then threaded the weight through the braid on his pole, followed by a plastic bead. When he tied the leader to the other end of the swivel (I had used a triple swivel with the extra eye not attached to anything), my rig was ready to go.

But at 5:00 a.m. the next morning when Scott came knocking on my rental RV, I sure as hell wasn't ready. I stumbled out and slugged down a can of Starbucks espresso, then followed Scott to his truck.

The night before I had stayed up till two in the morning, drinking and carrying on. With who? With my girlfriend—that's who! Because after a year and a half of being sad, I was now happy again. In fact, both of us, having gone through divorces and crappy relationships, were happy again. Now, however, it was looking like I was going to be hungover before the sun even rose.

Fifteen minutes later Scott and I were on the water and pulling away from the Cascades Locks launch, where a washed-up twelve-pound carp was attracting flies. A few minutes after that we were anchored in about fifty feet of fast-flowing river, twenty-mile-per-hour winds smacking at our windbreakers. Scott had advised two or three layers of sweatshirts to peel off as the day warmed up.

It took a few minutes of concentration for me to use Scott's worm-poking tool to thread a worm from one of my hooks to the other so that the worm was encasing the line between the hooks, and it wasn't a pretty sight. I had mangled my bait, but so what? I cast out and we both began to wait.

Three minutes later, "long-lining" off the bottom, Scott got a hit and reeled in two fish. One was a six-inch sculpin and the other was a ten-inch peamouth. He avoided touching the peamouth because of its cat-urine-in-a-closet smell (to paraphrase) and threw both fish back. Then I got my hit as well and reeled in a peamouth of my own. Then another. All morning long, peamouth after peamouth, ospreys flapping all around us, circling and waiting to dive, we kept catching peamouths.

The pikeminnow just weren't biting that morning, but Scott eventually connected with one. It was an inch too short. He threw it back, and we went to another spot, where the peamouths kept coming. I didn't feel much like plunking my weight if I didn't have to, because I tended to get snagged. Besides, the peamouths and sculpins were picking the bait off the bottom, so I figured pikeminnow would do the same. Meanwhile, the backdrop was magnificent: dramatic rusty yellow cliffs; gulls floating by; eagles soaring past the Bridge of the Gods. And sometimes there were dead fish floating down from somewhere upstream—injured peamouths thrown back by other pikeminnow fishermen.

But I finally got the bite that turned out to be a pikeminnow. And when I plopped it in the boat, only six inches long, I wasn't disappointed

FIG. 36. Spitzer and northern pikeminnow. Photo by Scott Foster.

at all. Nope! I had landed my targeted fish. It wasn't one I could turn in for the bounty, but that didn't matter.

What mattered was that I'd gotten it on a day that defied the odds, and back at camp, there was a smiley, beautiful, funny, imaginative, age-appropriate poet-professor waiting for me, with all her histories—and me with all mine on this bright blue day in which all of our pasts (including Scott's, and that of the entire northern pikeminnow fishery) were interconnecting in accordance with Chance. All this happening as the water flowed, as the wind blew, as the salmon populations that crashed in 2008 and 2009 swam upstream under us, making a comeback in their home.

The following morning *anamnesis* was the word of the day. An editor had sent it to my girlfriend (whose character I'll call Pescadora) as an editorial comment, because it's the type of word that makes people seem smarter than they are (which is why I'm using it now). I looked it up on my smartphone: "The remembering of things from another supposed previous existence."

"Wow," I said, "that's what I was just writing about."

The word *supposed*, however, prompted discussion. Figuring that all existences are supposed, I suggested that we all have numerous previous existences, just as fisheries do. The salmon and the northern pikeminnow demonstrate this perfectly; they existed together for eons until the dams, when the balance shifted. So now we're here, remembering things, evaluating things, and accounting for things in terms of earlier incarnations.

It was time to move on to breakfast. I had two tiny pikeminnows, the one I'd caught and another from Scott, and I wanted to know if they were really "poor table fare" as various sources attested. I'd cleaned them the night before, and the flesh was a bit mushy. The scales were troutlike and light. I had removed them, which might not have been necessary.

So here's what I did: I took those two gutted, headless fish and placed them on a bed of fresh thyme on a sheet of aluminum foil. Then I slathered them with chimichurri sauce and poured in some white wine for all this to sizzle in. Wrapping it up, I placed it on the campfire grill.

"If this doesn't make pikeminnow taste good," I said, "then nothing will."

Ten minutes later, it was time to put the fish to the test. I removed the foil from the fire, and when I opened it up, it smelled so damn good that I couldn't see how it could fail. After all, this food source had been used by indigenous tribes for centuries, though probably never in such a fancy quasi-Argentinean manner. Splitting both fish lengthwise down the middle, I pulled out the spines and removed the fins, knowing that even if the meat only tasted like the sauce, we'd be in luck.

Man, that fish was good! The texture wasn't even that lousy. Sure, it was bony; but those bones were soft and easily digestible. So take it from me and a much more credible doctor of philosophy who finished everything on her plate that pikeminnow makes great table fare.

FIG. 37. Pikeminnow station. Photo by Mark Spitzer.

I visited a couple of pikeminnow stations as well. The one at the Cascade Locks was basically a cargo van that came around in the late afternoon to register pikeminnow anglers for the next day's fishing and to collect fish removed from the system. The pikeminnow were counted up, thrown in coolers, and credited to the anglers' accounts, and at some point the checks would get mailed out.

The van/station at the Dalles was a bit more elaborate, no doubt due to the higher numbers of fish coming in. I found it there in the middle of the day, staffed by two workers. One was a young woman in her first year on the job, and the other was an older gentleman who'd been doing it for eight years. He was working on a laptop in the back, and they were both glad to answer my questions.

No, it wasn't that hot in the van, because there are usually strong winds blowing through the gorge. Yes, they sometimes take in a thousand fish per day. That's what they had been doing two weeks before, but today they'd accounted for only seventy-one. The Dalles is often on for the first two months of the season (May and June), but then the bite dies down, and no one knows why.

Then came the figure of four million, the older worker indicating that this was how many northern pikeminnow the program had removed from the system since 1990—a figure indicating that things are working out as envisioned.

There are plenty of reports and studies on northern pikeminnow vs. salmonids, but I still had a hard time finding anything that could support the conclusion that the Pikeminnow Sport-Reward Program, in collaboration with dam-site fishing, was actually helping the salmon populations recover and grow. Eric Winther, however, directed me to the reports webpage of pikeminnow.org, where I found the 2014 annual report on the Northern Pikeminnow Management Program. I kept skipping to the various evaluation sections, but for all the data collected in this 184-page whopper, it was difficult to find a sentence saying that the efforts were paying off. But I did find this: "Across all sites, abundance index values continue to remain lower than those calculated during years in which sampling was first conducted." This meant that pikeminnow densities were going down. Still, the information was scarcely a ringing endorsement.

So I chose a sample population to look at as representative of the overall crusade. I focused on the Bonneville Reservoir because the report said: "Abundance index estimates for 2014 in most locations sampled show a continued decrease in the number of northern pikeminnow greater than or equal to 250 mm FL in the Columbia River downstream of Bonneville Dam and in Bonneville Reservoir since the early 1990s." Table 3 in the appendix noted annual abundance index values like 8.5 and .86 in 1993 decreasing to 1.41 and .22 in 2014, and such figures seemed consistent across the board. These figures, though, spoke more to biologists and fisheries managers than your average angler on the street, and I kept coming across statements like "continued monitoring is needed to better understand the fisheries' association with the functional dynamics of the population."

I therefore decided to do some further investigating by going to the Cascade locks to interview salmon fishermen. That was where I found a number of vendors selling salmon from their trucks, parked by the side of the road. They were all Native American and glad to assess the situation.

The first place I stopped was called Joe Fish. Their fisherman was out in the boat, but his father was setting up coolers filled with fresh and smoked salmon. I bought some of the smoked and I asked him if the salmon fishing had picked up over the last few years. "The sockeye slowed down last year," he told me, "but the numbers are looking good for this year." He added that sea lions were becoming more and more of a problem by eating into the salmon populations. "But the salmon," he continued, "they have to adapt. That's nature. Salmon battle the elements, dams, sea lions, pikeminnows, everything."

I went over to the next table: Northwest Fish Hogs. They told me that even though there was a drought, they always did well. The spring run wasn't always the best, but the fall run was usually good, and things remained steady.

A block down the road, Brigham's Native Fish Market echoed the same sentiments about the fall run being better, but they added that "the run next year is not projected to be so good, because there's about six thousand sea lions now."

Moving on to recreational salmon anglers, I went down to the launch and approached some people fishing from the embankment. A fly fisherman told me the salmon fishery was picking up, and the last few years had been pretty good. Another couple of fishermen, sitting in lawn chairs with bells on their rigs, said things were average and that the sea lions weren't helping.

A guy bouncing a big pink lure off the bottom told me he'd been fishing this spot for thirty years and that salmon counts have gone up. He added: "Fall fishing is outstanding."

Thus the reactions were mixed. With my small sample of commercial and recreational salmoners defying consensus, though, one thing on which they seemed united was the fact that pikeminnow were only part of the battle for the salmon fishery.

A professional fishing guide later added to this perspective, telling me that the sturgeon he helps clients catch on his stretch of the system used to be a lot larger due to the amount of salmon that once occurred there. But throughout the last century there have been much fewer salmon in the river because there's a huge demand for their meat. Not only that, but now that there are more introduced predators in the river, more and more salmon smolt are being eaten by walleye and smallmouth, such that "sport fish" might even be devouring salmon more voraciously than the squawfish (a term he used in solidarity with others in the region who decline to accept the rebranding of *Ptychocheilus oregonensis*).

"I think that sport-reward program is just a feel-good thing," he said, "designed to make people think there's hope for salmon. But the fact is, this whole system has a lot to contend with, and you never know what will happen next."

Still, I hesitate to agree with the "feel-good" theory. The salmon numbers are there, and they're showing that after screwing up the balance of various freshwater species in order to reap the benefits of hydroelectricity, we are gradually making amends. And, in fact, we're doing it creatively—by actively creating incentives to get out there and thin the pikeminnow populations. And as I've already noted, predation of juvenile salmon is down by an estimated 40 percent.

But here's something else. We're looking ahead as we look back, which is important. Because if we don't take our previous existences into account, then that's the equivalent of not paying attention to patterns that have consequences. It's smart to account for the sturgeon crash of the 1890s, the recent West Coast salmon crash, all the cod crashes we've ever known, and all the other extinctions we could have avoided but didn't. And in doing so, we're sustaining salmon just as much as pikeminnow.

So as the sea lions move upstream more and more aggressively, and as the off-chance of a burbot blight descends as well ("you never know what will happen next"), the process of anamnesis is paying off in the Northwest. And even though I hate to say it, firm, pink salmon steaks are way sweeter and more succulent than bony, mushy pikeminnow meat, even with chimichurri sauce.

Conclusion

Grotesques of the West and Beyond

Without question, among the fish profiled in this book, the one that gave me the most trouble was the muskellunge. I kept after it, though, and after thousands of casts and thousands of dollars spent on gear and guides and travel, I met my next guide at his house in Clear Lake, Iowa. He was Kevan Paul, a good-natured young father with short hair and spectacles, and his boat was hitched up and ready to go.

We got out on the lake, which was 3,600-acres huge and contained at least two thousand adult muskies over thirty inches long. This fishery had been stocked for decades and was going strong.

The weather, however, was raining and gray and I'd forgotten to bring a raincoat along. We worked the shore, casting between the docks. I was using a black and chrome showgirl with a white rubber worm for a tail. All day long we cast and cast. The conditions were miserable and by the middle of the soggy afternoon, fatigue set in. My back was aching, we weren't catching anything, and the rain just wouldn't let up.

But in the last hour, the rain paused, and a silver flash slashed by the shore, curving like a crescent as it rose. It missed my lure, but we made a mental note of where it was. Then, when we came back to that spot fifty minutes later, after I'd surrendered to the fact that I'd just have to keep on hiring guides and casting past the point of exhaustion, it hit.

This time I was on it like lightning. I didn't give it a chance to fight, just cranked it in as fast as I could, refusing to let it turn or twist. Kevan lunged from his seat onto the deck, landed on his knees, and falling forward onto his chest, he plunged the net straight into the lake. I led the fish in and it was mine in less than five seconds flat.

The fish was 38.5 inches long and about fifteen pounds, a beautiful, green-sheened muskie with an orange tint on its tail. I couldn't tell if it was a spotted or a barred, and I didn't think to ask.

Kevan showed me how to hold the muskie, which was complicated, because it involved getting one hand inside the underjaw and curling the fingers to get a grip. Having forgone the gloves, my fingers instantly got all cut up by its razory inner-works and started bleeding—but so what? Kevan took a few shots, and we let it go.

Man, we were stoked! Having accomplished what I set out to do, I was glad to start heading back. But Kevan said the bite was on, so now it was time to get another, even if this made him late for dinner. And looking into his eyes, I knew what was up. He wanted another one for me, but he sure wouldn't mind getting one for himself.

We shot to the other side of the lake, where again we aimed our lures between the docks. On my second cast I saw a green and white human-sized head breach from the cabbage weed. This one was twice as large as the previous one, and it engulfed my lure right then and there, so I did the same thing, powering it in, giving it no slack, no chance to run at all. I yanked it in crazy-fast. Within three seconds I had it up next to the boat. Kevan dove again, lunging forward with the net.

Two seconds later we had that muskie on the deck, and it was a mon-ster. It had two huge parallel muscles busting from its back, and it was fatter than a soccer ball, forty-four inches long with ferocious fangs, and little wingy things protruded from its nostrils, positioned right in front of its eyes. We measured the girth to be almost two feet, which meant it was nearly thirty pounds, according to the muskie weight calculating chart I consulted later. It was the second biggest muskie Kevan had in his boat that summer, and we were high-fiving double-handed like football fans whose team had just won the Super Bowl.

FIG. 38. Forty-four inches, thirty pounds! Photo by Kevan Paul.

Like me, that muskie was bleeding. So after the money shot, I got it back in the water and held it till it swam off.

That was definitely the most directly rewarding moment in my odyssey of western grotesques, when all my failures to catch a fantastic and elusive fish finally paid off in a rush of success. Or was it? The time I spent on the Trinity in Texas, resulting in ten super-sized gator gar, was also unquestionably fine fishing—so why even try to decide which meant more? In a way, those muskies and those alligator gars played upon each other and built upon each other to epitomize the reason why we fish.

On this monster quest I was mostly alone with my own mind, driving thousands of miles, processing death and divorce, and these fish provided transcendental moments—the kind we live our lives hoping to achieve, the kind that reassure our chromosomes that Nature can save us from ourselves. And I can't stop thanking those fish for being there for me; as if they had a choice. As if we have a choice, when everything is an interconnected ecosystem of haphazard synapses clashing and glancing off each other in a world so incredible that you had better consider what you've got to lose. Because if you don't take a stand for what you love, then what sort of human are you?

Here's the problem. As our bleating, brainwashed masses are led astray by politically motivated deniers who create mis- and disinformation to serve their own purposes; as vital time is lost squabbling about what science cannot prove when science has never been a matter of opinion; as the growing seasons move north at the average rate of thirteen miles per day, and we find ourselves in the midst of a grave mass extinction; as the North and South Poles melt at the rate of 1 percent every year, and the top climate authorities are united on the fact that the polar ice caps will not exist in a century; as stubborn old-school holdouts continue to maintain that human activity cannot affect the environment—the whole fracking world is going to hell.

It might be fine if we were just wiping ourselves out. But to take fish and other species with us—that's an unconscionable, scurvy, self-destructive arrogance that pretty well justifies our own total extinction.

This, of course, is an inflammatory, grandiose statement. So sue me. Here are the facts. We've polluted the air with so much carbon dioxide that we are currently existing at an unsustainable level. The sustainable level is 350 parts per million, but at the time of this writing, we're at 400 and counting. This rise in CO_2 (up a third on our watch) has caused a 1.4° F change in global temperatures (EPA figures), with temperatures expected to rise as high by 11.5° F in the next century. Global droughts are intensifying and sea level is on the rise. As Elizabeth Kolbert notes in *The Sixth Extinction*, "If current trends continue, CO_2 concentrations will top five hundred parts per million. . . . It is expected that such an increase will . . . trigger a variety of world-altering events, including the disappearance of most remaining glaciers, the inundation of low-lying islands and coastal cities, and the melting of the Arctic ice cap."

And speaking of sea levels, all this carbon dioxide is souring the oceans. We are presently on the verge of a pH level of 7.8, and as Kolbert also notes, citing the research of marine biologist Jason Hall-Spencer, "the biggest tipping point, the one at which the ecosystem starts to crash, is mean pH 7.8, which is what we're expecting to happen by 2100." Since fresh water depends on salt water (plus the atmosphere and everything in it), and since fish depend on water, and since we all depend on water, we'd better get it together, people, or we're going to be bumming hard!

These were the inner rants that accompanied me as I drove, as I cast, as I sat waiting with bait in the rain, evaluating fisheries. But I still had another mission to accomplish: going after the most mammoth grotesque fish in the West. I'd caught white sturgeon before but nothing over four feet long.

So I signed up with Hell's Canyon Sport Fishing on the Snake River in Idaho. Why? Because the enormous white sturgeon pictured on their website were bigger than anyone else's in the region.

In mid-June Pescadora and I arrived in "Orwadaho"—where Oregon and Washington and Idaho meet. Ironically or not, we were driving a rental Great West Van, a ten-year-old clunker RV that had already blown one tire as it swayed its way from Seattle to Lewiston on shot shocks. It had a fridge and a bed and a kitchen and was itself a behemoth, but it was much uglier than the seven-foot sturgeon I was after.

At 5:30 a.m. we set out on the Snake, winding through the intense green-gold canyon cliffs and volcanic rocks jutting up from the rapids' froth. We saw deer on the shore and non-native chukar partridges from Eurasia in the willowy brush. According to our guide Jason Schultz, who'd been sturgeoning professionally for twenty-four years, the water was severely down due to drought. The Chinook numbers, however, were up, and the sturgeon were reproducing on this stretch, which wasn't happening in other places where dams had landlocked some populations permanently.

The boat was a twenty-eight-foot flat bottom that was about ten feet wide with lots of space for battling goliaths. It was powered by an inboard V8 and had a 9.9 Yamaha four-stroke for a trolling motor. As for gear, we had stout six-foot rods with golden baitcasting reels and 200-pound braided line. The hooks were barbless, and the weights were ten or twelve ounces.

First we had to catch our bait, which were gorgeous smallmouth bass, the exact same color as the mountains, but even more metallically irides-cent because they were wet. We caught them on light-weight spinning rods using crankbaits, five or six eight- to ten-inchers striking fiercely in the shallows. At one point Pescadora reeled in two bass on one lure at the same time.

Then we went to a forty-foot hole aswirl with some eddying action. Jason snipped the tails off two bass, then hooked them under the spine. I didn't ask why he did that, but I figured it was to limit their pull on the weights and to pump up their distress as they bled to attract pred-ators. He cast them out, then held us in place with the trolling motor, pointing downstream.

The first hit came and the tip of a rod started nodding. I was instructed to take that rod out of its holder but to wait for the next command. Jason then told me to reel in the slack, and since the tip was continuing to bounce, he told me to set the hook.

I hauled back hard and felt the weight. "Hit it again!" Jason advised. So I did it again and began cranking up.

Somewhere beneath me, something was resisting. It was one of the heaviest fish I'd ever fought, and sometimes it would take off. The drag would scream and the pole would flex. That sturgeon would go ten or twenty yards, but then I'd get a grip on it and haul back again, bringing in line when I lowered the rod.

This back and forth went on for about fifteen minutes, and I felt the strain in my spine. Fortunately, I had a lot of upper-body strength going on, having worked out at the gym for months, so I brought it in with minimal trouble.

A couple of times it rose next to the boat, and I'm sure it got a glimpse of us, because both times it freaked out and dove again. All the same I brought it back, and finally it just gave up and rolled over next to the rail, those weird, rubbery suction-lips and old-man whiskers pointing toward the sky.

Jason ran the bow up on the sand, and I jumped down. That fish was beached and lying there, totally mine and totally huge. It was six foot nine and 130 pounds, and it wasn't even eight in the morning when I nudged it back out to the Snake. We celebrated with Keystone Lights, which Jason kept on board because they sponsored his outfitting company. Still, this wasn't the fish I had come for, because it wasn't seven feet long.

It only took an hour for the next one to strike. This one I fought for at least twenty-five minutes. It dove and rose like the first fish, sometimes swimming toward us, other times peeling out thirty yards at a time. It wasn't quite as vigorous as the first one, but it had a lot more mass and a lot more determination not to be landed.

As Jason informed us, all these "big girls" (the larger ones being female) had been caught before, and some were over a hundred years old. There was even a ten-and-a-half-footer down there that kept getting caught, though he had not seen it in a while. Maybe it was dead, he figured, or maybe it was just getting smarter.

Whatever the case, the fish I had on turned out to be a back-breaker. I had to use the fighting belt to keep the rod's butt from digging into my pelvis, and we had a furious battle of wills. And when the fish finally came up, all three of us gasped. It was at least eight feet long, completely sharky, and studded with ivory scutes.

We ran it to shore, where I jumped out and sat down on it to make sure it couldn't flop away. I held it pinned to the sand as Jason came over with the tape measure. It was eight foot one and 250 pounds: the biggest fish I'd ever caught!

Now it was time to catch more bass, the bait they were hitting on. Sturgeon also bite on trout or salmon and other fish, but at this moment they preferred bass, and there were so many scrappy smallmouth competing in this system that it was legal to take as many as you wanted.

When the third sturgeon hit, I asked Pescadora if she wanted to take it. She said she was glad to just watch, but I knew the adventurous spirit in her that had taken me piranha fishing in the Amazon. It only took a couple of urgings, plus my lie that this one felt lighter than the first sturgeon, and she accepted the fighting belt.

I gave her the rod and somewhere in that eighty-foot hole a massive fish that was bigger and heavier than her began giving her the business. Still, she battled nobly, even when a passing boat created a wake that

FIG. 39. The big one! Photo by Jason Schultz.

knocked her to the deck. She fought the fish while rocking on her butt then moved to one of the seats. At one point the fish leapt, and we all saw its bright white belly in the air.

That sturgeon was burning her out, so after fifteen minutes I took over for about ten minutes while she regained her strength. She fought that fish again, and again Jason ran us up on the beach. She then led that 180-pounder up on the sand and leapt down after it—a complete victory! Not having fished since she was a kid, she'd gone from a seven-inch bass to a seven-foot sturgeon in just a few hours.

But as Pescadora told me later, "Mark, there's a difference between the way that men and women think about fishing. Guys want people to know that they caught a fish all by themselves, but for women, it's more about the community effort."

After that, we saw wild bighorn sheep and their lambs grazing on the mountainside and got right up close to them. We also saw an eagle that Jason had trained to dive for fish he tossed to it, and we spent the rest of the afternoon casting for bass to eat for dinner.

It pretty much blew my mind that during that whole day on the river we didn't see one other boat fishing for sturgeon. I mean, here we have a strong sport fishery for the most enormous freshwater fish on the continent—a beautiful grotesque, right there, right now, for the taking and releasing—but hardly anyone is taking advantage of this opportunity. That's what we've got, and that's who we are. That's what we need to keep around as long as we can. Because if we don't, the bottom line is we didn't try hard enough.

One more thing I had to do before sticking a fork in this book was to assess the 2013 Mayflower Oil Spill, in which more than 200,000 gallons of Canadian tar-sand crude had burst from a ruptured pipeline and glooped its way into Lake Conway, where I live. Since I ended my last fish book with the message that we need to keep a close eye on our resources to protect them, it was now time to find out what sort of carcinogenic mutagens were being absorbed by *our* fish, which are *our* responsibility. Because all the fish we pollute, all the fish we compromise—we are responsible for their health just as much as for the health of everything in the food web we take for granted.

Basically, if I found these fish were polluted, then I was ready to start writing letters to editors and press releases about toxicity levels and safety concerns. And if I found that the adage "dilution is the solution to pollution" was true, I'd emerge with a more optimistic conclusion for this book.

This was a job for Fishing Support Group. I called a meeting to take on this mission, and we launched right by the culvert where the spill had gone into the lake. Half of that petrochemical goulash had sunk to the bottom, escaping the booms and backhoes ExxonMobil had sent to collect the residue.

With Turkey Buzzard and Minnow Bucket in one canoe, and with Scotty in the other with me, we set out about four dozen jugs and noodles baited up with minnows and worms in an area where the bait shop guy had spotted an alligator. We didn't see that gator, but by sunset we had two good specimens: a two-pound largemouth and a three-pound channel cat. I figured they had grown up in the spill and represented a good sample, since bass pretty much share the same diet as crappie, and catfish pretty much share the same diet as gar and drum and other fish I typically eat from this body of water, and these fish were your typical eating size.

Turkey Buzzard, however, lost the stringer, giving us all good cause to make fun of him until we caught another bass and another cat. Those fish were wrapped up in multiple layers of tinfoil and newspaper and plastic and delivered to Analab Corporation in Kilgore, Texas, which tests for the various toxins that the Arkansas Department of Environmental Quality had detected at elevated levels: benzene, isopropylbenzene, total xylenes, anthracene, benzo(a)anthracene, benzo(a)pyrene, pyrene, and the metals barium and silver. I also put in a request to measure mercury and lead levels, since these contaminants show up in fish all over the country due to coal-burning power plants.

The homogenized wet-weight results came back a month later, and they were surprising. Analab tested for everything I asked for plus a couple of dozen additional toxic chemicals for each fish. So I sat down for a beer with Turkey Buzzard, aka Dr. Robert Mauldin from the

Chemistry Department at the University of Central Arkansas, and we went through the results. The only contaminant with detectable levels in either fish was barium. In the bass, barium measured 0.561 mg/kg, and the amount in the catfish was almost ten times greater, 6.8 mg/kg.

"So it's safe to assume," I asked, "that 'undetectable levels' mean that these fish are clean?"

"Yep," Turkey Buzzard answered, "but it depends on the barium."

I emailed Dr. Jacob J. White, associate professor of chemistry at the University of Rio Grande, and put the barium question to him. His reply:

> According to the Agency for Toxic Substances and Disease Registry, the minimum risk level for both intermediate- and chronic-duration oral exposure is 0.2 mg barium/kg bodyweight/day. This is also the same as what I found from the EPA as the reference dose for barium, so there are two reported references levels that are in agreement (which is good, and not always the case). I could find no reported acute toxicity determination (I found several references indicating that this has not yet been determined). What this reference level means is that a person can consume up to 0.2 mg of barium for every kilogram of body weight every day with no likely adverse health effects due to its consumption. Your results from both the catfish and bass fall below this threshold, showing little/low danger from barium. To determine this, I made two calculations assuming a 150-pound person consumes one 8-oz filet each day. This calculates to 0.0227 mg Ba/kg/day for your catfish sample and 0.00187 mg Ba/kg/day for your bass sample, both falling well below the reference level of 0.2 mg/kg/day.

There I had it: results I didn't expect at all. The fish were clean. I didn't have to raise the alarm. Even better, I could return to running the trotline I'd abandoned two years before, and I could eat fish from Lake Conway and not worry about glowing in the dark at night.

Testing those fish gave me hope that sometimes things fix themselves. But obviously things can't always fix themselves, and when they can't, we need to be proactive before the fecal coliforms hit the fan.

It's not just a matter of stocking systems with more fish. First of all, stocking may be good for sustaining specific wildlife populations, but it's not always cost effective or even possible for some economies. Second, hatchery-raised DNA mixing with wild strains leads to less genetic diversity in fisheries, which weakens entire ecosystems. Third, we have evidence showing that other approaches have tremendous potential, and we'd be fools to not make use of that research. But ultimately, just as financial advisors recommend investing in a wide variety of stocks and bonds and annuities, it's advisable for us to put our eggs in multiple baskets rather than betting on a single prospect. Let's face it: the problems we are facing now are too complex to address primarily by stocking particular species. We need to address the issues on multiple fronts.

What we need is imagination—ideas to debate, and models to test, showcasing ideas that work so that they can be applied to other fisheries.

And we are being imaginative. We're doing this with American eels in Arkansas and beyond, by experimenting with specialized ladders to aid in migration. We're being imaginative with burbot as well, using fishing tournaments in Utah and Wyoming to stabilize the destructive numbers. To sustain sturgeon populations in the Northwest, we're limiting annual harvests and requiring barbless hooks. In the case of spoonbills, we're mixing paddle-sperm and paddle-eggs with turkey feathers in Missouri to give a highly compromised species a boost in a highly compromised system. For Asian carp in Kansas and the rest of the country, we're starting to envision how our tax dollars can be better spent, and how we can exploit this proven food source.

Meanwhile, mass muskie propagation models for catch-and-release fisheries are working well in Minnesota and Iowa, and we're being creative with gator gar in Texas, where we're using helicopters to search for and rescue stranded gator gar. Collecting wild razorback larvae through annual roundups in Arizona and Nevada is an imaginative approach that's proving effective in reclaiming the lost range of this native endangered species, and so is placing a bounty on northern pikeminnows, which is gradually resulting in a more balanced salmon fishery from Oregon to Idaho. Then there's bowfin, which (according to Dr. Solomon

David at the Shedd Aquarium) we're beginning to reimagine in terms of function, especially in relation to northern pike, gar, and other fish and their movements through agricultural channels. This research is just beginning, and I hope some research on conserving the genetics of massive flatheads will be seriously considered based on my challenge to create game preserves for jumbo cats.

Of course the problem is large. We've got a planet going down, so we need big ideas really fast, minus the unconstructive bickering and annoying delays that fritter our natural resources away. Luckily, we are a nation of creative thinkers, as our history of innovation underscores. So let's continue with that tradition, and apply our most ingenious ideas to the future.

Ideas having to do with algae are a good place to start. "Iron fertilization," or feeding the Antarctic Ocean with iron particles to trigger the growth of blue-green blooms that absorb CO_2 and sunlight is one idea being discussed, as is the fact that we already know how to produce a greener gasoline by growing algae (the original fossil fuel) in giant vats. Other forms of imaginative geoengineering include the "monochrome Earth method," in which the idea is to paint roads and roofs white in order to reflect sunlight back into space. Diane Ackerman's *The Human Age* notes a few offshoots of this approach, including "covering the deserts in white plastic, and genetically engineering crops to be a paler color. . . . Or installing roof tiles that turn white in hot weather, black in cold. More bizarre tech fixes include firing trillions of tiny mirrors into space to form a hundred-thousand-mile sunshade for Earth, or building artificial mini-volcanoes that spew sulfur dioxide particles into the atmosphere to block sunlight. There's even been a 'modest proposal' that we genetically engineer future humans to be tiny so that they'll need fewer resources."

Abuse of petroleum is the biggest problem on this planet next to overpopulation. Every time we burn a gallon of that heroin, we churn out 5.1 pounds of carbon into the atmosphere. Those little black specks are too small for us to see with the naked eye, but they absorb sunlight and fuel global warming. The production of natural gas and ethanol requires fuel to create fuel; it's just not practical to create a barrel of oil by burning more than the same amount, which is what we're doing. It makes sense to keep investing in wind, geothermal, and other alternative energy sources—and especially solar, because, as the poet Amiri Baraka observed, "Who need fossil fuel when the sun ain't goin' nowhere"?

And as Al Gore pointed out in a 2009 Senate Foreign Relations Committee hearing, citing research from *Scientific American*, "if we took an area of the Southwestern desert 100 miles on a side, that would be enough, in and of itself, to provide 100 percent of all the electricity needs for the United States of America in a full year." Similarly, biologist Len Ornstein has documented that foresting the Australian Outback and the Sahara Desert would absorb all the carbon dioxide that the world spews into the atmosphere every year.

Then there's the working theory of mariculture, which offers a way to burn a lot less oil on farms and in other food-producing industries by growing crops vertically rather than horizontally. As Ackerman writes, "if you created a network of small seaweed farms around the world that add up to the size of Washington State, you could feed the whole world." As she informs us, "kelp photosynthesizes, but not just the leaves, the whole kelp. As a result, it pulls five times more CO_2 from the air than land plants do. . . . The Department of Energy did a study that showed if you took an area half the size of Maine and just grew kelp, you could produce enough biofuel to replace oil in the U.S."

As the journal *Scientific American* established in 2009, "Wind, water and solar technologies can provide 100 percent of the world's energy, eliminating all fossil fuels." The authors of this article, Mark Z. Jacobson and Mark A. Delluci, indicate that we have the knowledge to go completely green in two decades—meaning there's no need to keep ruining the environment. Similarly, in regard to the idea of "pioneering bioneering," to quote Ackerman again, "We billions of creative, problem-solving humans don't have to be parasites in our environment—we have the technology, the understanding, and the desire to become ecologically sustaining symbionts."

Here's another challenge, in the spirit of my challenge to the noodling community. Let's get as creative with our solutions for our fisheries as we are with the biggest problems we face on this planet, because it all boils down to one thing: we're burning through our resources at a suicidal rate. We're a species with blinders on, in denial of the fact that other species on this planet are vanishing at the rate of nearly two hundred per day. If the world goes to crap, it says a lot about our character if we at least tried to prevent that.

So who are we going to be? The people who accepted our excesses and died out for the luxury of the one-percenters, or the visionaries who saw a complex set of problems and set aside the BS to get down to business in the name of biodiversity? Because here's the thing about biodiversity: we need it. There are three main reasons to keep as many different types of life around for as long as possible, according to the recent groundbreaking United Nations report *Connecting Global Priorities*:

Biodiversity, food production and nutrition: Biodiversity is the basis for crops, livestock and farmed fish and other parts of agricultural production and aquaculture. Genetic diversity within these ensures continuing improvements in food production, allows adaptation to current needs and ensures adaptability to future ones including climate change . . .

Microbial diversity and non-communicable diseases: Humans, like most living things, have a microbiota—ecological communities of commensal, symbiotic and pathogenic microorganisms that literally share our body space and outnumber our human cells ten to one. The majority of these microbes provide vital functions for human survival. . . . Reduced contact of people with the natural environment and biodiversity, and biodiversity loss in the wider environment, leads to reduced diversity in the human microbiota, which itself can lead to immune dysfunction and disease . . .

Infectious diseases: Biodiversity plays a complex role in disease emergence, with benefits in some contexts and threats to human health in others. Human changes to and degradation of ecosystems, such as modified landscapes, intensive agriculture and antimicrobial use, may increase the risk of infectious disease transmission.

This information comes from the *United Nations Environment Programme* website, and was reviewed by Brandon Kelm on NPR's *Science Friday* on July 17, 2015. As Kelm noted, this report demonstrates that biodiversity is necessary for the protection of human health, because the fewer organisms you have in a system, the more "crash and boom" species you have. It's easier for us to get sick when we depend on fewer species; the more organisms we have in a system, the more back-up we have to take it for the team (my words, not his) when it comes to infectious diseases.

So if we want to preserve ourselves, let's be *self*ish in the most generous way possible: by focusing on preserving links in chains that sustain human life.

Most of us feel powerless, and are in effect powerless, when those who can make the difference have other priorities. But at a community or state level we can work together on our fish. I'm living proof of this, as are all the guides and activists and specialists I met in this investigation. They know that taking care of fish is another form of taking care of ourselves. And in taking care of ourselves, we take care of the world.

The book ends with the image of me paddling my stripy green and yellow canoe. It's seven in the morning; there's a green heron in the channel continuously hopping into the air and leading me out to the lake. The lily pads open and the path is clear. Turtles pop their heads up and just as quickly disappear. I enter the main lake, and the shad are plipping on the surface.

The night before, we had a party. Turkey Buzzard and his wife Brandy paddled out in a flat-bottomed boat and spread twenty noodles throughout the cove, baited with trotline minnows. Buzzard's son Anthony, just back from Afghanistan, was in a canoe with Minnow Bucket, who was hanging hook-lines on my trotline strung across a submerged creek. I'd set that line earlier, and it was already bringing in some catfish.

Pescadora and I worked our way down the trotline in another canoe, rebaiting hooks with goldfish and sunfish before we all paddled back to my place and barbecued a rack of ribs.

Now, checking my trotline in the morning, there are three new catfish on. They're a gleamy, golden speckly brown, but since I have a bag full of fresh fillets sitting in my fridge, I throw them all back except the last one, which seems to be calling to me. *Please, dude, let me go. Come on, be a sport* . . .

I take a closer look. It's not that old, only a couple of pounds, but it's been through a lot. There's a scuff on the back of its head where the skin is rubbed off, and it also has an injured lip, where I suspect it was hooked before. With its bugging bubble eyes and Gothic whiskers, its wide mouth and bulging gut, this ugly fish is definitely a "beautiful grotesque."

These words contradict each other, which, of course, is the point: the combination sets up an ironic tension. But "beautiful" and "grotesque" also complement each other, and this truth is embodied in the fish I hold in my hand: it is as just pretty as it is hideous. It's a hardy fish of the American West, stocked all over the continent; it sustains itself well, reproduces easily, gets along with other species under all sorts of adverse conditions, and it contributes to its environment. It's also widely farmed because it's an excellent, dependable food source.

So I let it go, back into the lake where Turkey Buzzard's missing pink noodle is still out there somewhere, being towed around by a fish big enough to pluck a ten-ounce weight off the bottom. It might be a mammoth buffalo, or freshwater drum, or a big old blue or flathead cat, or a fugly bowfin. It might be the state record spotted gar, or a shortnose, or a longnose, or an invasive species.

The possibilities in these western waters are just as myriad as our grotesques, which will hopefully always accompany us. Because grotesques are human constructs that we create from the depths of our imagination, and the thought of them amuses us, educates us, informs our future. So if you see a pink noodle on the run, chase it down and haul it up. But be prepared to find way more than just a fish. And if you land a beautiful grotesque, it's yours. And you can keep the pink noodle too.

Notes

INTRODUCTION

2 "We go eastward to realize history": Henry David Thoreau, "Walking," *Atlantic Monthly*, June 1862.

2 *Cadillac Desert* documentaries: *Cadillac Desert: Water and the Transformation of Nature*, directed by Jon Else and Linda Harrar (Columbia TriStar Television and PBS Home Video, 1997).

5 That thesis, later published: Mark Spitzer, *Bottom Feeder* (Creative Arts Publishing Company, 1999).

1. NATURE OF THE AMERICAN EEL

11 "influenced by environmental factors": "Endangered and Threatened Wildlife and Plants; 12-Month Finding on a Petition to List the American Eel as Threatened or Endangered," U.S. Fish & Wildlife Service, Department of Interior, 2007, http://www.fws.gov/policy/library/2007/07-429 .html, date accessed June 13, 2014.

12 I'd read in James Prosek's: James Prosek, *Eels: An Exploration from New Zealand to the Sargasso, of the World's Most Mysterious Fish* (HarperCollins, 2010).

14 "dams and natural waterfalls": U.S. Fish & Wildlife Service, Department of Interior, *Federal Register*, vol. 72, no. 22, February 2, 2007.

22 And it's also too late: Douglas Main, "Decision Looms on Fate of Declining American Eels," *Newsweek*, September 15, 2015, http://www.news week.com/decision-looms-fate-declining-american-eels-372467, date accessed March 12, 2016.

22 "have the broadest diversity": U.S. Fish & Wildlife Service, "American Eel: *Anguilla rostrata*, *fact sheet*, September 26, 2011.

2. ENVIRONMENTAL LEMONADE

30 95 percent of the participants: Monica Lundquist, "Cass Sheriff, Commissioner Concerned with Eelpout Mess," *Brainerd Dispatch*, April 2, 2013.

31 "trash, garbage, and human waste": Lundquist, "Cass Sheriff."

34 "Frogs . . . Q-tips": Rob Buffler and Tom Dickson, *Fishing for Buffalo* (University of Minnesota Press, 2009), 21.

34 "544 metric tons of crayfish": Chris Lueke, quoted in Ryan Mosley, Burbot Summary 2011 (unpublished report), Utah Division of Wildlife Resources, 2011.

3. URBAN STURGEON

46 As a commercial fish: Richard Adams Carey, *The Philosopher Fish* (Counterpoint, 2005).

53 "one thinks of the sturgeon": Howard T. Walden, *Familiar Freshwater Fishes of America* (Harper and Row, 1964), 275.

53 Witnesses alleged spotting monster sturgeon: "Iliamna Lake Monster," *Wikipedia*, https://en.wikipedia.org/wiki/Iliamna_Lake_Monster, date accessed February 17, 2014.

55 maximum length for the species: *Audubon Society Field Guide to North American Fishes, Whales and Dolphins* (Knopf, 1983), 365.

57 white sturgeon eat: Bud Connor, *Great White Sturgeon Angling* (Frank Amato Publications, 1996), 10.

57 University of California's fish website: http://calfish.ucdavis.edu/species /?ds=241&uid=113, date accessed February 17, 2014.

57 "worms, and considerable plant material": *Montana Field Guide*, http:// fieldguide.mt.gov/detail_AFCAA01050.aspx, date accessed February 17, 2014.

57 "a half bushel of onions": Walden, *Familiar Freshwater Fishes*, 275.

57 "is one of the great mysteries": John Waldman, "The Lofty Mystery of Why Sturgeon Leap," *New York Times*, October 21, 2001.

58 "artificial propagation of this fish": Walden, *Familiar Freshwater Fishes*, 276.

58 "extracted from the sturgeon": California Caviar Company, http://www .californiacaviar.com/our-caviar/domestic/main.php, date accessed February 17, 2014.

4. SNAGGING IN THE OZARKS

63 "consumer willingness to pay": *Paddlefish & Sustainable Aquaculture*. www .paddlefishfarming.com/about.html, date accessed March 24, 2014.

64 "True, the negroes of the South": Jordan and Barton Warren Evermann, *American Food and Game Fishes* (Doubleday, Page and Company, 1902), 3.

66 locals contacted the department: "MDC and Federal Agents Snag Major Paddlefish Poaching Operation," mdc.mo.gov/newsroom/mdc-and

-federal-agents-snag-major-paddlefish-poaching-operation, date accessed December 1, 2013.

66 "The national and international popularity": "MDC and Federal Agents Snag Major Paddlefish Poaching Operation," mdc.mo.gov/newsroom /mdc-and-federal-agents-snag-major-paddlefish-poaching-operation, date accessed December 1, 2013.

67 The Missouri Wildlife Code: Missouri Department of Conservation, *Code of State Regulations*, Chapter 6, 3 CSR 10-6.525 Paddlefish, January 29, 2014, http://www.sos.mo.gov/adrules/csr/current/3csr/3csr.asp, date accessed December 1, 2013, 9; U.S. Fish & Wildlife Service, International Affairs, "Lacey Act," http://www.fws.gov/international/laws-treaties-agreements /us-conservation-laws/lacey-act.html, date accessed December 1, 2013.

68 "The story of sturgeon": *Sturgeons and Paddlefish of North America* (Kluwer Academic Publishers, 2004), vi.

68 "poor water quality": University of Arkansas Press, http://www.uapress .com/dd-product/the-scars-of-project-459/, date accessed May 2, 2014.

69 "Artificial stocking sustains": Missouri Department of Conservation, press release, February 25, 2014, http://mdc.mo.gov/newsroom/great-things -ahead-paddlefish-snaggers, date accessed May 2, 2014.

73 when these paddlefish reach an arm's length: Carlye Adler, "Caviar from the Heartland," *Fortune Small Business*, October 24, 2006. Republished in *CNN Money*, http://money.cnn.com/magazines/fsb /fsb_archive/2006/10/01/8387305/, date accessed March 24, 2014.

74 "a growing interest": John Jerome, "Polyodon spathula: American Paddle- fish," *Museum of Zoology Animal Diversity*, http://animaldiversity.ummz .umich.edu/accounts/Polyodon-spathula/, date accessed March 20, 2014.

5. ALIEN INVADERS IN THE WEST

78 "in a protracted, increasingly violent conflict": Austin Alonzo, "Fighting Flying Fish: Company Dredges Up a Hazard," *Kansas City Business Jour- nal*, March 28, 2014.

87 "Asian carp have not": Dave Golowenski, "Don't Fear Asian Carp, OSU Professor Says," *Columbus Dispatch*, September 5, 2010.

89 A commercial industry: Jim Gallagher, "Let Them Eat Carp: Illinois to Feed Pest Fish to the Poor," *St. Louis Today*, July 14, 2011, www.stltoday .com/business/local/article_9492759b-5968-5021-9c13-23168664f0d3 .html, date accessed September 19, 2013.

90 "The trouble is": Jackson Landers, "How to Stop an Invasion of the Eas- iest Fish in the World to Catch," *Slate's Animal Blog*, November 18, 2013, http://www.slate.com/blogs/wild_things/2013/11/18/asian_carp_in_great _lakes_call_them_silver_fin_and_eat_them.html, date accessed April 1, 2014.

6. NEBRASKA BOWFINS AND BULLHEADS

100 "The spelling 'grindal' was used": *Bowfin Anglers' Group*, http://www.bow finanglers.com/bowfininfo.html, dates accessed May 1, 2014, January 26, 2006.

101 "the ecological role": Jonathan G. Davis, "Reproductive Biology, Life History and Population Structure of a Bowfin *Amia calva* Population in Southeastern Louisiana," thesis, Nicholls State University, 2006, 8–9.

104 The fish shown: *Michigan Fishing*. http://www.fishweb.com/recreation /fishing/fishfacts/fish/yellow_bullhead/, date accessed May 1, 2014.

7. FEAR AND NOODLING IN OKLAHOMA

116 "Every year," he said: Bradley Beesley, quoted in "Catfish and Controversy at the Okie Noodling Tournament," *Gastronomica* vol. 11, no. 2, 2011.

130 "The unprecedented use": Zeb Hogan, "About Megafishes Project," http://environment.nationalgeographic.com/environment/freshwater /about-megafishes-project/, date accessed July 5, 2014.

130 "results are in the noodlers' favor": Heather Alexander, "Texas Family Members Are Champion Noodlers Once More," *Houston Chronicle*, June 25, 2014.

8. MUSKIE HUNTING IN MINNESOTA

138 The editors: Josh Stevenson, "I, Muskie Hunter," *Field and Stream*, June 2014.

9. VISION QUESTING GATOR GAR IN THE SLICK TEXAS MUD

148 "9,200 alligator gar": "Alligator Gar Research in Texas Helps Protect Trophy Fishery," *Texas Parks and Wildlife*, August 11, 2011, http://tpwd.texas .gov/newsmedia/releases/?req=20110811a, date accessed May 11, 2014.

148 "Texas is the best place": *Texas Megafish Adventures*, http://www.texas megafishadventures.com, date accessed May 11, 2014.

149 It sought to debunk: Mark Spitzer, *Season of the Gar: Adventures in Pursuit of America's Most Misunderstood Fish* (University of Arkansas Press, 2010).

150 My second book: Mark Spitzer, *Return of the Gar* (University of North Texas Press, 2015).

154 "gar thrive in the Mississippi": "How to Fish for Alligator Gar," *Wikihow*, http://www.wikihow.com/Fish-for-Alligator-Gar, date accessed May 11, 2014.

10. RAZORBACK ROUNDUP AND RECOVERY

166 In fact, by 2010: "Xyrauchen texanus," *The IUCN Red List of Threatened Species*, www.iucnredlist.org/details/23162/0, date accessed March 2, 2015.

167 thirteen wild razorbacks: Zachary Sattuck, Brandon Albrecht, and Ron J. Rogers, *Razorback Sucker Studies on Lake Mead, Nevada and Arizona: 2010–2011 Final Annual Report*, Lower Colorado River Multi-Species

Conservation Program, U.S. Department of the Interior, Bureau of Reclamation, October 2011, 1.

181 "In the Lower Basin": Hillary Rosner, "One Tough Sucker," *High Country News*, June 7, 2010.

182 humpback suckers "are detritivorous": *Animal Diversity Web*, http://animal diversity.org/accounts/Xyrauchen_texanus, date accessed March 3, 2015.

182 "What we do is fundamentally": Chuck Minckley, quoted in Craig Springer, "Rounding up Razorbacks," *Endangered Species Bulletin*, September–October 2000.

11. ALL HAIL THE PIKEMINNOW BOUNTY

185 "Their primary diet": Scott Foster, *Pikeminnow Rewards* (Amazon Ebooks, 2013), 4.

187 "to reduce the average size": "Background," http://www.pikeminow.org.

187 "cut bait (strips cut from fish)": Samuel L. Calvin, *Catch Northern Pikeminnow: Earn Thousands on Your Summer Vacation* (Mercedes Publishing, 2005), 17.

187 Histand earned over $20,000: Mark Youasa, "Columbia River Northern Pikeminnow Final Reward Program Top Angler Earns $77,238," *Seattle Times*, November 4, 2012, http://blogs.seattletimes.com/reeltimenorthwest/2012/11/04/_nikolay_n_zaremskiy_of, date accessed June 20, 2015.

191 Still, a weight of 13.5 pounds: *Encyclopedia of Life*, http://eol.org/pages /210298/details, date accessed June 20, 2015.

191 cites a figure of twenty-eight pounds: *Fishing World Records*, http://www .fishing-worldrecords.com/find?findByCountry=USA, date accessed June 20, 2015.

197 "Across all sites, abundance index": Steve Williams, "Report on the Predation Index, Predator Control Fisheries, and Program Evaluation for the Columbia River Basin Experimental Northern Pikeminnow Management Program," 2014 Annual Report, Pacific States Marine Fisheries Commission, 60.

CONCLUSION

203 "If current trends continue": Elizabeth Kolbert, *The Sixth Extinction* (Picador, 2014), 113.

203 "the biggest tipping point": Jason Hall-Spencer, quoted in Kolbert, *Sixth Extinction*, 118.

208 I ended my last fish book: Mark Spitzer, *Return of the Gar* (University of North Texas Press, 2015).

212 Other forms of imaginative geoengineering: Diane Ackerman, *The Human Age* (Norton, 2014), 53–54.

213 And as Al Gore pointed out: Alexander Lane, "Al Gore Is Optimistic about Solar Energy, and Pretty Accurate, Too," *Politifact*, http://www

.politifact.com/truth-o-meter/statements/2009/feb/18/al-gore/al-gore
-optimistic-about-solar-energy-and-pretty-a, date accessed March 14,
2016.

213   Similarly, biologist Len Ornstein: Ackerman, *Human Age*, 54.

213   "Wind, water and solar technologies": Mark Z. Jacobson and Mark A.
Delluci, "A Plan to Power 100 Percent of the Planet with Renewables,"
Scientific American, November 1, 2009, http://www.scientificamerican.
com/article/a-path-to-sustainable-energy-by-2030, date accessed March
16, 2016.

214   species on this planet are vanishing: John Vidal, "UN Environment
Programme: 200 Species Extinct Every Day, Unlike Anything Since
Dinosaurs Disappeared 65 Million Years Ago," *Huffington Post*, August 17,
2010, http://www.huffingtonpost.com/2010/08/17/un-environment-pro-
gramme-_n_684562.html?utm_hp_ref=green, date accessed July 17, 2015.

214   there are three main reasons: Secretariat of the Convention on Biological
Diversity and the World Health Organization, "Report on Health and
Biodiversity Demonstrates Human Health Benefits from Protecting Biodiversity," *UNEP News Centre*, February 14, 2015, http://www.unep.org
/newscentre/default.aspx?DocumentID=12818&ArticleID=11139, date
accessed July 17, 2015.

215   this report demonstrates that biodiversity: Brandon Kelm, *Science Friday*,
NPR, July 17, 2015.

IN THE OUTDOOR LIVES SERIES

*Pacific Lady: The First
Woman to Sail Solo across
the World's Largest Ocean*
by Sharon Sites Adams
with Karen J. Coates

*Kayaking Alone: Nine Hundred
Miles from Idaho's Mountains
to the Pacific Ocean*
by Mike Barenti

*Bicycling beyond the Divide:
Two Journeys into the West*
by Daryl Farmer

*Beneath Blossom Rain:
Discovering Bhutan on the
Toughest Trek in the World*
by Kevin Grange

*The Hard Way Home:
Alaska Stories of Adventure,
Friendship, and the Hunt*
by Steve Kahn

*Almost Somewhere: Twenty-Eight
Days on the John Muir Trail*
by Suzanne Roberts

*Stories from Afield: Adventures
with Wild Things in Wild Places*
by Bruce L. Smith

*Beautifully Grotesque Fish
of the American West*
by Mark Spitzer

To order or obtain more information on these or other University of
Nebraska Press titles, visit nebraskapress.unl.edu.